INTEGRATING MONEY AND MEANING

Practices for a Heart-Centered Life

To a life of meaning and joy. I love! — Maggie

MAGGIE KULYK
with Liz McGeachy

Integrating Money and Meaning
Practices for a Heart-Centered Life

ISBN 978-1-7337322-0-8

www.chicorywealth.com

For my beloved brother Mark

Contents

Introduction

This fish was bigger even than any whale we know—as big
as a mountain!—and it had an equally enormous appetite:
it ate and ate and ate until it had eaten all the food left in
the kingdom. And then it roared at the king for more!
—EAST AFRICAN LEGEND OF KING
  SULEMANI AND THE WHALE

The image of a leviathan so enormous it can devour
people, ships, even entire kingdoms, can be found
throughout the world's mythology and literature. In
many of those stories (Jonah and Pinocchio come to mind),
people exist inside the belly of the colossal beast, perhaps
unaware of their captivity, much less imagining any avenue
of escape.

In my many years working in the financial industry, I've
thought of this image often. Like King Sulemani's whale,
our money system—at least in the Western world—is truly
colossal, encompassing every economic, social, industrial,
and cultural structure that makes up our complex society.

And like Jonah and Pinocchio, we exist inside this daunting money system, often unaware of how it surrounds us and affects not just our daily tasks but also our inner spirit and the spirit of our communities.

I see the effect of living inside this whale every day when I interact with my clients around money. People are worried, stressed, confused, angry, occasionally joyful, but more often fearful when it comes to money. The plethora of seminars, self-help books, and websites promising relief from this kind of anxiety attest to its prevalence in our culture.

Unfortunately, this mammoth system is not going anywhere. In fact, each day it grows larger. The web of institutions and policies we've created to interact with money grows in complexity, lack of transparency, and the ability to create haves and have-nots. This web, in turn, props up just about every other aspect of society, including politics, the environment, research, education, religion, food, health, entertainment, art—the list is endless. Nowhere is this rampant expansion more apparent than in the outcome of the 2016 United States presidential election, when a billionaire businessman/reality TV show host with no experience in politics squeezed his way into becoming the leader of the "free" world. Money doesn't just talk—it shouts.

"Get Up and Deal with Your Money"

Angst around money has certainly been a part of my own life, even though—and partly because—I grew up in a family with plenty of it. Even as a kid, I was aware that while money certainly bought options, it did not deliver happiness. Throughout this book I offer stories from my own life, as well as the lives of others, that exemplify how money's tendrils reach into every pocket of our being, starting when we are very young. I do this because I think it's helpful to hear stories about how these theoretical issues can play out in the world, but also to bring them out of the shadows and into the light of day. If we can't see where we are, how can we change where we are going?

For now, I'll describe my situation at the age of thirty-seven, when I found myself at a crossroads. At that time, I had been in and out of my family's business several times and sold out my portion of the company, only to lose most of the money in a crazy business venture. I'd also seen one important relationship in my life end and another begin, adding children to the mix. I had made a career switch and attended divinity and graduate school, then found the doors of that career path closing, too. In many ways, my life was in utter shambles, but I had done at least one thing right. I had added a well-known spiritual practice to my daily routine, meditation. Though I was new to the practice and my mind raced frantically through every short sitting, for some reason, I stuck with it.

One day as I sat on my cushion, I seemed to be wrestling more than usual with my unruly thoughts, most of which were worries about money. Then out of the blue, the waters of my mind calmed and a message emerged: "Get up and deal with your money." At first I resisted, trying to force the river of my meditation in another direction. This couldn't be "right"—money and spiritual practice don't mix. But soon I stopped resisting, and the message became clear: "Get up and deal with your money."

After the meditation session ended, I lingered over what had just happened. It seemed important, so I decided to listen. I began by looking realistically at my own financial situation and making changes. Later, I took the trainings necessary to help others do the same. I love this work, mainly because I believe I'm helping people relieve some of their stress and fear around money. God knows most people need help navigating the guts of this crazy beast—budgeting, investing, asset management, protection, goal-setting, long-range planning, and so on. Advocating and helping at such a fundamental level is noble work. Nevertheless, at times I feel like a doctor in a MASH unit, just stitching up the wounds of an ongoing war. We are in the belly of the beast, and it's acidic down here, folks.

That's the dark side of the story, but there is another side. My own personal life experiences and my experiences working with others have shown me that it is possible to live inside our money system without being utterly consumed by it—to live within it and still find a level of peace, balance, and wisdom—to find meaning. Though it is not the norm, I have met people with that level of health, and it has little to do with how much money they have. These people intrigued me. I wanted to know how it was that they were able to thrive in this environment with what appeared to be relative ease. I examined this phenomenon, and the answer that emerged was a spiritual path. All of these people had some sort of spiritual practice—but not just that. There are many people who consider themselves to be on a spiritual journey, but I noticed that these people included money on that path. Learning how to do that is the purpose of this book.

What Is Spiritual Practice?

Before I go further, I want to say a little bit about the concept of "spiritual practice." This is a broad term used loosely in our culture, and it means many things to many people. For some, such practice is connected with a particular religion, while for others it's not. I include both in my concept of spiritual practice, as long as the practice is regular and intentional (thus, the use of the term *practice*) and originates from a desire for deeper union with what I call the divine, but others may call unconditional love, a power or mystery greater than the individual person, or the great connection between all. In short, the point of spiritual practice is to train the heart toward love—both giving and receiving—and for the wielding of love's power.

There are many avenues to spiritual practice, and I will suggest some of them in this book. They're generally focused on the individual, and the goal is individual transformation. But ultimately, spiritual practice relocates one's egocentrism in a broader context through empathy and interconnectedness with others. Spiritual practice is a way of being in the world that contributes not just to personal peace and equanimity but also to community healing and health through love, compassion, and mercy. In fact, you can't really have one without the other.

Why add money to the spiritual path? I believe the answer is twofold. First, recognizing and naming the power and influence of "the whale" can help us alter that power and influence to some extent, so we can live within it in a more balanced and healthy way, both physically and emotionally. It is possible to find meaning there; we are not powerless.

This honesty and deep practice can be at times painful, but ultimately it offers the opportunity to be more at peace in our money lives, and in our lives as a whole. But there is a second, larger consequence of adding money to the spiritual path, beyond that of reducing individual stress. Dismissing or denying the money system's power feeds that power, but spiritual transformation feeds a higher good beyond the system's focus on individualism. Through practice, we can learn to relate to the world in a broader, more meaningful and deeply healing way, even though we may continue to live inside the leviathan. We may not be able to live outside this system in a practical sense, but we can dwell outside it in this spiritual sense. It's my belief that, ultimately, individual spiritual transformation influences—in both small and large ways—the greater world. In other words, if our own hearts change, *the heart of the whale changes too.*

What This Book Is and What It Isn't

This book is partly about my own journey of "getting up and dealing with my money," a journey that will no doubt last the rest of my life. But it's more than that. I believe it offers a way for people to move beyond the angst or "dis-ease" that many have around money. I have been talking about the subject of money and spiritual health with people for many years now, and though at first the connection between the two may feel unfamiliar, it resonates deeply. No matter how much money people have in the bank or their retirement fund, or whether they grew up in a mansion, a one-room cabin, or somewhere in between, most have a complex and emotional relationship with money—often accompanied by deep wounds. What we

have, and what we believe about what we have, greatly influence the decisions we make about how we live our lives and
who we think we are—in other words, how we live inside the
whale. Yet despite the enormity of its influence, we don't talk
about money much, except maybe at the dollars-and-cents
level. To the extent money is discussed, it's often considered
practical, mundane, even crude—not for polite company.

With this book, I offer practices that can help bring money
out of the shadows so it can be realistically faced. This includes
looking at the role money has played in our lives and the lives
of those who raised us, recognizing our personal tendencies
and dysfunctions around money, and being up front about
money's personal symbolism for us and how we use it to shape
our lives and the greater society. Becoming clearer about
our experiences and wounds around money is the first part
of this spiritual practice, but the second part flows naturally
from the first. With practice, we can create new relationships
with money based on our true "hearts," which naturally lead
to connections to others and the wider community. The second part of the book offers practices for strengthening that
connection.

There are plenty of books out there about money, so let
me be clear about what this book is *not*:

- This book is not "money enlightenment in 10 easy
  steps" or "make $100,000 in two weeks or less," or
  anything remotely similar. This book is *not* about how
  to make more money, but instead about being more at
  ease in a world dominated by money. I will go even further to say that this book is not for people experiencing

poverty. This is a dire problem in our society that desperately needs to be addressed, but those specific answers are not here. While I believe spiritual practice will benefit anyone, this book assumes that readers have access to a basic level of privilege, in that they are able to sustain themselves with a roof over their heads, food, and clothing.

• I must admit that this book does not provide easy answers. In fact, it will likely leave the reader with more questions than answers and perhaps a sense of discomfort. But that is part of the "practice." The hope is that this discussion and the practices I offer can help people start on a journey toward a new relationship with money, and ultimately with themselves and others.

• This book is not an opiate to help us feel better about or deny our society's monolithic, complex financial system or to escape it altogether by going "back to the land" or "off the grid." Getting off the grid may be an option for a select few, but not many. Instead, this book offers ways to honestly address the power and immensity of our financial system and its effect on us. In doing so, I believe we can feel less daunted by the system and learn to find a meaningful connection with this system.

• This book is not just for religious people. I do think people of many religious backgrounds will find this book meaningful, but it is not inherently Christian, Buddhist, or derived from any religion at all. Those who find themselves yearning in any way for the divine, the great mystery, a creative energy that connects all beings, a power greater than themselves, the deepest soul within themselves—all will find a perch here.

- This book does not preach a "prosperity gospel." Though I do believe looking in depth and with honesty at our lives through the lens of money can help us prosper, I don't define this by the accumulation of more money. If that is the goal, there are better books out there for guidance, although I will say, in the end I believe they will disappoint. Money should not be confused with emotional, physical, and spiritual health.

- This book does not provide nuts-and-bolts tips for financial planning, budgeting, or investing. There are professionals out there who help do that. What it will do is help you approach money with an open, unencumbered heart so that money can play a deeper role in your life and in society as a whole.

CHAPTER 1

Living in the Whale

Money often costs too much.

—RALPH WALDO EMERSON

A Money Story

The little one-stoplight town where I grew up in Erie County, Pennsylvania, had been a bustling little village in the earlier Bessemer Railroad days, but its sheen had begun to tarnish by the time I came along in the early 1960s. There were still a few small businesses in those days—a bank, a couple of grocery stores, a barber shop, plenty of bars, and churches of course. A few remaining Victorian homes, many built by my grandfather and his two brothers, lined the two parallel main streets that were both crossed by the railroad track running straight through the middle of town.

The surrounding countryside had at one time been covered with forest, but by then, a lot of it had been converted to farmland. This is the part of Pennsylvania that begins to flatten and bleed into the Midwest, and the town had a somewhat Midwestern sensibility. But there were also a fair number of transplants from the coal country of West Virginia, and in some ways, it represented the northernmost tip of Appalachia. There weren't many opportunities for work, and there wasn't much to do.

If you think I'm painting a bleak picture, you would be right, and the place grew gradually bleaker as the 1960s faded into the '70s and '80s. Nevertheless, my family's manufacturing business continued to thrive. The business was in my mother's side of the family, with its heyday during the two world wars. By the time I was born, things had slowed somewhat, but the business was still a main employer in town and provided a decent living for the unionized skilled laborers who worked as welders and steel fabricators in the manufacturing plant. The business was profitable, and as a result, my family was quite affluent—unlike most of the residents in town. We lived in a large ranch house perched on several grassy acres just outside of town. A big back deck with a stone fireplace looked out over the yard and barns. I was the last of four children, with six years between my closest sibling, Mark, and me. The span was twenty years between the eldest and me.

My mother was always involved with the business, but less so when she was raising young children. In 1956, with two young teens and the assurance from her doctors that she could not have any more children, she was eager to reengage. Imagine her surprise, then, when along came my brother Mark, throwing in the proverbial monkey wrench. Not surprisingly, when she became pregnant with me six years later, she was not any happier, and Mark and I both experienced the repercussions of this unhappiness. Of course, it wasn't all bad for Mark and me. My parents' affluence was peaking by then, and we were raised with an enormous amount of privilege compared to my older two siblings, and certainly compared to the folks around us. We had more "stuff" and traveled more than our other siblings ever did. My mother was incredibly generous to the wider community and in her support of various charities, but she had a harder time at home. I know I am not the only person born to a mother whose intelligence and ambition were thwarted by an unwanted pregnancy. Still, the knowledge (whether conscious or unconscious) that your mother doesn't really love you—and in fact, at times seems to truly resent you—takes a lifetime to overcome.

Despite the interruptions of pregnancy, my mother was the chair of the board of the family business. My father acted as CEO, but had only one share in the business itself. Family dinners were often spent with my parents arguing over the business. My mother had come to own the business after her elder brother and her father had a falling out—over money. The story I was told involved blackmail, kickbacks, and an ugly court case, culminating in my uncle (whom I never met) leaving the business and becoming estranged from his parents and his only sister and her family. It left a huge rip in the family fabric, and the story was told often as a cautionary tale when I was growing up: to be "like my uncle" implied disloyalty, entitlement, and even criminality. There seemed to be no line between the business and the family.

My mother's side of the family was very different from my father's. My mother lavishly took care of her mother,

Margaret—for whom I am named—while Margaret managed to make every day a living hell for my mother, as far as I could tell. She visited us every Sunday, sitting in the living room in her jewelry and furs, sipping tea from her favorite china. The tension in the house was palpable. Margaret was fussy and difficult, and she hated that I was called "Maggie," referring to the nickname as "pig-in-the-parlor Irish." By contrast, my mother's father was held in high esteem, though he died before I was born.

On the other hand, my father was a first-generation American, his parents having come to the United States from Eastern Europe in the early 1900s. Mark and I and all our cousins on that side of the family loved visiting Baba and Zeezee (which roughly translated from Ukrainian means "old woman and old man") in their tiny wood-frame house, complete with garden, compost heap, chicken coop, and fishing pond. Zeezee had shoveled coal for the railroad, but he was long since retired and ailing by the time I knew him. Baba was an expert gardener and grew zucchini the size of baseball bats. I couldn't communicate with them well because their English was limited, but the vibe in their house was sweet and loving, and the food was excellent! Chicken soup with homemade noodles, pierogi stuffed with potatoes and fried in onions and butter, halupki (cabbage rolls), homemade bread with honey.

My father was the middle of five children, and it was clear to me at an early age that he was the star of his family. He had married into wealth when he married my mother, and he worked his way up from a sweeper of floors to the president of the company. He was helped along certainly by his marriage, but also by his drive, ambition, and native intelligence. He had a kind of gutsy confidence, and while not arrogant, he seemed to truly believe in himself and his self-worth. He was very attractive as a young man (a reality not lost on my mother) and had, to his dying day, a kind of personal magnetism. But perhaps his greatest business attribute was that he never feared failure.

As a consequence, under my father's leadership and the help of a strong economic cycle favoring infrastructure spending, the family business thrived, and my immediate family grew rich. Though this affluence did nothing to promote healthy relationships, it did allow my mother to hire a nanny for me, a woman named Ann. In fact, some of my sweetest, early memories are not of my mother's love, but the love of my brother Mark and the love of a nanny with whom I became deeply bonded. Ann came from a similar ethnic background as my grandparents and was about their age when she was hired by my family. As a toddler, I followed Ann around like a little duck as she went about her daily work, doing laundry, making beds, ironing clothes, and preparing food. She would travel with us when we went on trips as a family, all of which seemed to revolve around the business. My parents would go out, wining and dining potential customers, while Mark and I stayed with Ann.

When I was about four, Mom, Dad, Mark, and I went on a brief overnight trip to Cleveland. It was a short trip, and for whatever reason, Ann did not come along. I remember crying inconsolably because she wasn't with us. It was as if strangers had taken me away on a trip and wrenched me from my mom. They had to call her on the phone and let me talk to her to calm me down. Soon after we returned, I remember waiting in the kitchen for her arrival. I was talking to my mother, describing a card game I hoped to play with Ann that day, and she responded, "Ann is not coming here anymore." I stopped, feeling as if a hole in the earth had opened and swallowed me. I looked out the kitchen window and stared at the rolling lawn and barns that sat below the house. I don't remember speaking or crying, but at some point, I heard my mother say, "Your dad fired her." I didn't know what "fired" meant, but I understood the finality in the tone and knew my life was forever changed.

As it turned out, my father was upset by my bond with Ann. I learned later that there were already tensions between my father and Ann, but when he saw my reaction at being separated from her, his response was to fire her. My reaction to her loss was so intense I actually buried it in my mind. I would be in my twenties, driving down the highway taking a drag off of a cigarette, when I suddenly remembered her. I had so deeply denied the painful memory that I had completely forgotten her existence, and it hit me like a freight train. I burst into tears remembering my forgotten "mother." I never saw her again.

Ann was the source of my early nurture, and along with my Baba and Zeezee, the foundation of a working-class sensibility that would never fully leave me. With my parents, though, I could never quite connect. One afternoon when I was about fourteen, I was lying on the couch when my father came in and dropped a piece of paper on my chest. "I thought you'd want to know your net worth," he said and walked out. I don't remember exactly what was printed on the paper, but it was several hundred thousand dollars, which meant almost nothing to me. But I could tell he was happy about it. I'm sure for him this was a gesture of love and support, showing me how well he was taking care of me. But it only left me feeling alienated and confused about the sum total of my "worth."

Eventually in high school, I got involved in athletics and found my feet, even a few friends. I began to differentiate from my family background and be seen on an individual basis, rather than just a member of my family (and the business). But an underlying residue of discomfort around money lingered. I remember driving my mother's banana-colored Cadillac through town one day, supposedly on my way to mass, but I just kept driving. I was thinking about money—my family's money—and how it felt like a stone tied around my neck that I wanted to throw off. I had no clear direction and no sense of limits, and I was terrified.

This is the beginning of my story living inside the belly of the whale. Everybody's story is different, of course, but we all have one. I offer this as an example of how those stories can be viewed through the lens of money. We rarely do this, but money's influence is everywhere, whether we choose to recognize it or not. In my own story, money affected the character and vibrancy of the town I grew up in, my family's business, the people who worked for that business, my relationship with my mother and father and others, and pretty much every choice I made along the way. I don't mean to imply that this was the *only* influence on my life and my choices, but it certainly was a part of the story, including my confusion between my "net worth" and my "self-worth." These influences should not be ignored.

What Is Money Anyway?

We tend to think of money as cut-and-dried: the bills in your pocket, a number on a statement, maybe a pile of coins sitting in a vault somewhere. But money is anything but cut-and-dried. It's a slippery metaphor and hard to pin down—and it has its own story.

Money's Birth

At its inception, "money" was simply a medium of exchange. Before money, people bartered or traded goods and services. "If you give me that raccoon hat, I'll chop some firewood for you or give you some of my grape harvest when it comes in"— that kind of thing. But when people wanted rabbit instead of raccoon or were tired of waiting around for the fruit to ripen, they began using symbols of this trade. As early as 2200 BC, people used shells, stones, beads, and fur in this symbolic process of trading or bartering. The first coins were used to facilitate this process around 600 BC when the Lydians, in what is now Turkey, began using gold and silver coins for the purpose of commerce and giving people access to a whole new range of goods and services. Soon the Greeks and the Romans were getting in on the action, becoming more sophisticated with the addition of moneylenders and other entrepreneurs to allow for debt and credit. These changes in how goods and services were exchanged also created changes in society and how people related to each other. It opened up more free time for some, allowing them to pursue the arts, sciences, and religion, producing the classical era of antiquity. Of course, free time for some meant bondage and slavery for others. Money was shaping society.

The Chinese moved from coins to paper money in the early centuries, and by the time Marco Polo traveled there in AD 1200, he was amazed to find paper money. Paper money (or bank note IOUs) didn't become prominent in European countries until the seventeenth and eighteenth centuries. Like the shift to coins, the shift to paper currency also affected society. It allowed for easier international trade, banking, and the financing of wars and exploration. From this grew stockholder-owned corporations and institutions controlling access to money, which birthed the complicated system we have today around debt, interest, taxes, insurance, the value of currency, and the legalities related to it all.

Money's Complexion

Today money is no longer simple—not by a long shot. It has grown far beyond coins and paper bills. It's even outgrowing credit cards and checks. I read the other day that wallets are on their way out. Who needs one? With the rapid growth in technology, "money" is now handled through phones and other electronics, so that currency is now mostly virtual. The system has grown so invisible it's easy to forget that money is—or at least was, at its infancy—just a medium for facilitating trade.

Charles Eisenstein, author of *Sacred Economics: Money, Gift, and Society in the Age of Transition*, says, "Money is just an agreement. Money only has value because people believe it has value."[1] We believe in this value because money does indeed give us access to the things we need (food, clothing, shelter), but we often carry this belief into a perception that money also provides status, happiness, and fulfillment. It works because we buy into this agreement.

I like Joe Dominguez's definition in his best-selling book *Your Money or Your Life*. He calls money "something we choose to trade our life energy for."[2] Whether we like it or not, in our culture we exchange our personal time and energy for money so we can get what we believe we need and want for ourselves and our family. We get it—even though the price is often our own depletion.

There's actually an innate biological reason why we do this. Though we like to downplay the fact, we humans are biological creatures shaped by our natural attributes. The goal of all creatures is survival for the individual and for the species. To survive in our culture, we need at least a certain amount of money. Let's face it: How many of us, if push came to shove, could grow our own food, build or heat a home, or provide basic health care to ourselves or loved ones? Maybe a few, but not many. Our parents perhaps, or our grandparents, might have had a few of these skills, but most of us today are way down the supply chain when it comes to providing basic needs. We've moved beyond the *Little House on the Prairie* days when Ma and Pa could go into town now and again to buy or trade for gingham or coffee, but survive for the most part on their own wits and strength, rather than money.

This connection to survival is of course one of the reasons we are willing to "trade our life energy" for money. It's also the reason money can stir up such strong feelings of fear and uncertainty. For even the most confidently independent of us, down there in the muck of our basic animal psyche is the message, "If I don't have 'enough' money, I and those who depend on me will die." And like any animal facing such fears, we can be triggered into a fight, flight, or freeze response. We all know that if we're walking in the woods and a tiger lunges toward us, this instinctual response will kick in, and we'll either fight back, play dead, or get the hell out of Dodge. The same thing happens with our fears about money. If we perceive that things are not going well for us moneywise, the old reptilian brain kicks in: we freeze, do nothing, pretend it's not happening. Or we may flee into alcohol, drugs, food, sex, or spending. The fight response might cause us to work harder and harder to make more money and incessantly guard our assets. Awareness of these responses may not be as apparent as when we run from a tiger, but they are there.

We value money because it helps us survive, but money goes one step further. Money divorces us from that very reality—you know, that pesky idea that one day we will *not* survive. Intellectually, we know that as natural beings, we will eventually die, but we don't like that idea much. Money helps us put off that inevitability and deny our mortality, or at least we pretend it does. This is such a predominant characteristic of money that our whole financial system is built on it: the idea that we can escape our mortality by denying our animal nature and our connection to the natural world.

A prime example of this disconnect is our economic system's unwillingness to take into account the externalized costs of goods and services—the debit we make every day to the natural world through our purchases. We pay our water bill and think nothing of where it comes from, what it takes to assure that it is clean, or where it goes and what it does after leaving the drain. We treat the natural world as if it were an indestructible and infinite ATM machine on which to draw, and our monetary system embraces this kind of false accounting system. This denial of our connection to the natural world is part of the complex nature of money. Money helps us survive, and that's a good thing. But at the same time, it disconnects us from our place in the natural world.

The Shadow Side

It's clear that money has "value" because it helps us get the things we want, including our own survival. Most people initially think of money in this positive way. But money also has a negative side, which is certainly not a new concept. Think of that classic definition of money as "the root of all evil," for instance. Many of us were brought up on this reference from the Bible, but we need to quote it correctly. In the Bible, 1 Timothy 6:10 actually says, "For the love of money is the root of all evil." Money isn't necessarily the problem. It's our *love of money* or our *relationship to it*—whatever that may be—that gets us into trouble. That relationship often carries with it the baggage of fear, guilt, anxiety, greed, idolatry, shame, control, power, even violence. The Bible may name this "evil," but I prefer to call it "the shadow side," a much less loaded term. It implies that we—instead of being bad or evil—have multiple sides when it comes to money (and everything else for that matter), including a dark side that we tend to hide from ourselves and the world. Addressing this side and being honest about it can enlighten us, if we let it. The trick is to acknowledge it with nonjudgmental compassion.

When it comes to us and money, we all have our shadow sides—negative emotions that money triggers. It's "natural" to want to feel secure and unafraid, so we use money to help us get to that place of security. But the truth is, we will never be completely secure. It's part of being a human. The more we are unwilling to face this aspect of our humanity and money's complicated relationship with it, the larger and more powerful our money shadow side will grow.

This reminds me of Isaac, a little shaggy black mutt I once owned. Isaac was a "Katrina dog"—one of thousands of pets separated from and never reconnected with their original owners (if they had one) during the hurricane that hit New Orleans in 2005. Isaac was about a year old when my family adopted him, and we didn't have any information about his first few months of life. Likely though, he'd seen more than his fair share of trauma. At times, Isaac could be playful and even affectionate, but more often he was aggressive and irritable. He was what those in the pet biz call an extreme "resource guarder." You didn't dare go near him if he was around his food, his toys, or anything else he considered his own.

Isaac wasn't bad or evil, but he had a tremendous shadow side. Resource guarding in dogs is instinctual, since they evolved from scavengers competing for food and other resources. Guarding food in particular was critical for survival. Over thousands of years of domestication, dogs have evolved so they don't need to resource guard so much. But that instinct is still there, and for a few dogs, it becomes a prominent characteristic. Whether it was a trait Isaac was born with, something he learned early in life, or both, he never got over it, even though we tried many forms of training and interventions during his years with us.

When it comes to money and the things that money can buy, most of us have at least a little bit of resource guarding in us, some more than others. It's natural, even instinctual, to guard what we need to survive. The shadow side emerges when we—like Isaac—take our resource guarding too far. On some level, we are doing this to avoid facing our own mortality, but mostly we have lost sight of or have never known what's actually needed to survive. We have no idea what's "enough." Most people in our society have enough money to cover their basic expenses. Yet a vast majority believe they don't, or are filled with fear that they won't. They believe, if they have just a bit more, they will no longer have those fears and will be happier. But studies don't back this up. It is true that if you do not have your basic needs met (say, you're in the lowest 20 percent of national income) and you get an increase in income, this *will* likely make you happier and less fearful. But above that threshold, more money doesn't make much difference in happiness. In fact, it may have the opposite effect.[3]

Social psychologist Paul Piff has studied the relationship between wealth and compassion. He looked at numerous studies that included thousands of participants across the United States. He and his colleagues found that as a person's level of wealth increases, their feelings of compassion and empathy go down, while feelings of entitlement and an ideology of self-interest increase. These studies showed that wealthier individuals are in general more likely to moralize greed as being "good" and see the pursuit of self-interest as favorable and moral.[4]

Money's shadow side can also show up as the opposite of resource guarding: denial. We all know people who, for whatever reason, do not handle their money realistically. They spend it with abandon—either on themselves or others—without thinking of the consequences. This is an example of an out-of-control, reptilian flight response, and can cause as much angst around money as the opposite.

It's ironic that in the United States—the richest country in the world—most people who have their basic physical needs met are awash with fear and anger and other negative feelings when it comes to money. And, of course, these feelings spill over into our relationships with others. The shadow side can rear its head when we're around people we perceive as "different" from us. Perhaps we see them as having a lot more money than we do, or a lot less. Or we see them spending or saving their money differently than we do. We wonder whether they're judging us, or maybe we're judging them. We resent them because they seem to have "everything" and we don't. Or we're afraid they feel that way about us. We wonder if we should be helping them, and we feel guilty if we're not. Or we help too much and resent it, or worry about ourselves. We may have some of these feelings about our own family members as well as those we don't know so well. We don't like this state, and it produces more anxiety, more discomfort, more "dis-ease."

Personally, I see this "dis-ease" in not just biological or psychological terms, but theologically. I believe we are created with a divine-shaped void that we long to fill. Not everyone may use these same terms or express this theologically, but I think many would agree that humans experience a deep emptiness that cannot be explained away simply by upbringing or circumstances. There is a longing to address this void, but most of us don't know how to recognize it, much less fill it. I'm certainly not the first person to describe humanity's innate discontent this way. St. Augustine of Hippo, 400 AD, said in *Confessions,* "You have made us for yourself, O Lord, and our hearts are restless until they rest in you."[5] And Blaise Pascal said this in 1670 in *Pensées*:

> What else does this craving, and this helplessness, proclaim but that there was once in man a true happiness, of which all that now remains is the empty print and trace? This he tries in vain to fill with everything around him, seeking in things that are not there the help he cannot find in those that are, though none can help, since this infinite abyss can be filled only with an infinite and immutable object; in other words, by God himself.[6]

Whether we use the word *God* or *the divine* or *love* or *the deepest mystery,* the point is that we are beings who have within us a longing for a relationship with ultimate reality. We try to fill it, but the void is easily distorted. Sometimes we fill it with junk that doesn't satisfy: Twinkies, martinis, the "perfect" vacation, sex, risky sports, computer games, extreme working hours. The list goes on and on, and our consumer society is cunning in its ability to play into that need—feeding the shadow.

Let me give you just one example of how this worked on me. A few years ago there was an ad on TV showing a family holiday gathering. Everyone was visiting and relating to each other, happy as can be, except for the one checked-out teenage son who wouldn't get off his phone. As I had teenagers at the time, I thought, "Yeah, that's just like my kids. They don't care about the family. They only care about their electronics and their games and their own friends." But at the end of the ad, the teenage son takes the phone and plugs it into the TV, showing everyone gathered around a beautiful video of his family that he's secretly been creating over the holidays with his fancy phone. People laugh. People cry. They hug each other. They understand how much he really loves his family, and guess what? He's creative to boot. He'll probably even win a college scholarship with all that creativity! I have to admit this ad sucked me in. I immediately went out and bought the phones in the ad for each of my kids. Why? I want my family to be happy. I want to have fun holiday gatherings where we all laugh and hug each other. I want my kids to want to be around me *and* to be creative and make something beautiful. What can magically make all that happen? The answer, according to this ad, is that particular phone. Only after I made the purchase did I begin to be honest with myself that the outcomes I was hoping for had nothing to do with the phones.

Money touches all these parts of us—biological, psychological, and spiritual. It does so in both positive and negative ways, and mostly in ways that live in that murky area between the two. The trick is not to deny any of the ways money affects us, but especially those ways that are hiding in the shadows. Otherwise, the shadows grow.

Life in the Whale Today

We are living in interesting times, my friends, no doubt about that. As I write this, billionaire businessman and TV reality show host Donald Trump is president of the United States, unrolling his very money-influenced agenda. His election to the presidency was a surprise to many, but in hindsight, perhaps it shouldn't have been. Money has always influenced politics and every other corner of society, but that influence is growing exponentially. The election of this particular president indicates how true that is, as well as something more sinister. It represents a growth in our societal shadow.

I don't mean to make this entirely about one person, but instead what he symbolizes for all of us right now. Deepak Chopra, founder of the Chopra Center for Wellbeing, noted this in an interview with Fox Business News in March 2016 during the US presidential campaign:

> He [Trump] represents a state of collective con- sciousness of fear that has dormant prejudice and hatred. He is inspiring that in those people that it already exists but is lying dormant, and he is the catalyst for bringing it out. So this is a moment of sobriety for all of us to see that this is part of our dark side. ... He represents our shadow. He represents our collective shadow that includes you and me because there is no one who doesn't have a shadow.[7]

We all have that shadow side, and our monetary and political systems do too. That shadow side is growing due to our refusal to accept and confront this side of ourselves. In fact, we are normalizing the shadow and reframing it as "good." I refer again to the studies done by Paul Piff, who found a greater tendency in people to accept self-interest and greed as "morally good" the more money they had. This dangerous transformation is happening before our eyes in this country.

Though he uses different terms, author Tim Wise also identifies this change in the moral reference points of capitalist societies today. In his 2015 book *Under the Affluence: Shaming the Poor, Praising the Rich and Sacrificing the Future of America*, Wise cites a growing sense of "cruelty" or "Scroogism" toward the poor.[8] There was a time, Wise reminds us, when the majority of people looked with sympathy and solidarity on struggling people in need. In today's culture of severe and growing income inequality (the chasm between "rich" and "poor"), the message tends to be contempt and personal blame toward people in poverty. Wise argues that this change in direction has been created and perpetuated by personal entitlement linked with surfacing racism. Rather than a culture of community, we have become a society of individuals wanting our "due." Those with privilege are the "winners," and by privilege, I'm referring not just to financial wealth, but to race, education, physical health, sexual orientation, and so on. If you are privileged in these arenas, you have a huge head start toward "success." And though all these elements are part of the measure of success in our society, money has become the number one measure of accomplishment.

The society I'm describing is built on the underlying belief that we all need, want, and deserve endless abundance. Money is seen as the tool for living our fullest lives (and therefore the lack of money is an impediment to this). But this premise is based on a false illusion, an unattainable mirage. The inevitable consequence of living with this mirage is anything but abundance for everyone. Instead we have excessive abundance for a very few, and barely enough for many others. Civilization has not seen the extent of income inequality we see today since the Gilded Age, and it is truly stunning. The wealthiest eighty-five people on the entire planet have more money than the poorest 3.5 billion people combined. It's hard to even take in that statistic. Between 1979 and 2007, the wages of the top 1 percent of households in the United States rose ten times more than the bottom 90 percent. And when incomes decline during an economic downturn, the gap continues to widen. During the recession of 2007–09, for example, the average wealth of the top 1 percent dropped by 16 percent; meanwhile the wealth of the bottom 99 percent dropped 47 percent. The statistics go on and on and are startling.[9]

Overall, this side of life in the whale is pretty grim. Many find it easier to focus on the positive aspects of life in our financial system (and there are plenty) than to admit the harsh realities. Meanwhile, our tremendously distorted monetary system does extreme damage to the planet and to the human beings who inhabit it. And it's under stress. The path we're on as a nation and a world is not sustainable—either in terms of the ways we extract resources from the environment or the ways we extract human energy to uphold the system. For the most part, we do these things without counting the costs, but eventually the bill comes due.

From "Dis-ease" to "Ease"

Though I've painted a bleak picture of life inside our whale of a financial system, I do so with purpose and with hope. The purpose is to speak honestly and openly about our current situation without shrinking from it or sweeping it under the rug. This is a critical first step in making changes to the growing system. I do not live under any illusion that this system is going away, but I do believe one can live within it with a stronger sense of health and well-being than most people do. I know people who do this, and I have personally experienced growth away from the "dis-ease" of living within the system. This gives me hope. The more people who are able to navigate the system with a sense of spiritual well-being, the better it will be for the system as a whole.

Moving from spiritual dis-ease toward ease when it comes to money is the focus of the rest of this book. This will necessarily mean talking in a real way about money. This may seem obvious, but in fact, most people are uncomfortable talking about money. If I were to ask a group of people at an event to share their latest tax returns with everyone in the room, they would be horrified. Most would more willingly talk about what they did in the bedroom the night before than divulge their finances. A survey of 2000 millennials done in early 2017 found that 39 percent of participants said they would rather disclose a preexisting sexually transmitted disease to a potential partner than reveal their debt.[10]

This secretiveness around money adds fuel to the fire of angst and pain in our relationship to it and gives it power. Nowhere is this more prevalent than in our spiritual lives. As I described in the introduction to this book, when I felt during my meditation the need to "get up and deal with my money," at first I resisted; this had to be a mistake. In our society, we have a money life and a spiritual life, and never the twain shall meet. Ask churches or nonprofit organizations trying to raise money for their work. To use the technical term I hear some of them use about fund-raising: "We hate talking about money. It's icky."

But being honest about money—the good, the bad, and the icky—is exactly what we *must* do if our goal is wholeness on a personal level and in the wider world. And I am not just talking about discussing our feelings about money with a counselor or a close friend, although of course this is a good start. Excavating and examining our relationship with money and our struggles around it in an effort to align our money lives with our spiritual lives must become among the most important practices of our age. Not only will this alignment benefit our relationship with money, it will reach every corner of our lives.

CHAPTER 2

Looking Back

Rather than love, than money,
than fame, give me truth.
HENRY DAVID THOREAU

W hen it came time for me to go to college, I chose to go to a state school (to the annoyance of my mother). My father discussed with me how much I would need to live on. Neither of us had a clue about an appropriate amount. However, we agreed on a sum that would be sent to my checking account every month. Soon I began to accumulate money in my account and asked him to reduce the monthly amount. I didn't enjoy spending money on myself, though I did enjoy buying for others. But it also made me anxious because I had no idea what things should cost. I began to feel a terrible tension between having too much money and not having enough, at the same time recognizing that none of the money was really mine to begin with. While my parents never said so outright, I could feel the strings.

In college I started to become politically active. I was surrounded by people barely making it and having to work two jobs to pay for school. That was obviously not the case for me, and it made me uncomfortable. To make matters worse, the tradition in my family was to receive a car of your own in the summer between your freshmen and sophomore year in college. For once, I was clear about what I wanted—a Honda—and I told my parents. I thought Hondas looked cool, I'd heard they drove well, and I knew it would blend in. What did my father buy me? A BMW. Again, I was caught. I didn't want to seem ungrateful or spoiled, so I acted thrilled, and on one level, I was. It was a beautiful car, and it drove well. But naturally it stood out on a campus such as mine, and once again, I felt "outed" by my family's wealth.

Two weeks before I was to graduate from college in 1985, the family business held a gala in honor of its eightieth anniversary in my hometown. I didn't want to go, but my parents told me I had to be there because they didn't want to explain my absence, and I obliged. The weather on the day of the gala was odd. It poured rain in the morning then became very humid, hazy, and unnaturally warm by midday. It made me feel strangely tired and ill, so I lay down on my childhood bed to take a nap. Suddenly my mother ran into the room, yanked me off the bed, and screamed, "Tornado!" We ran toward the basement, and as I looked out the sliding glass doors, I saw about two hundred yards away trees bent to the ground and their tops lopped off and blown away.

We crouched in the basement, fearing for our lives, until the destruction was over. Miraculously, our house was still standing, but the F5 category tornado had ripped straight through the middle of town, killing at least twelve people and destroying about 150 buildings and homes. Gone were the Victorian houses along the main streets, reduced to kindling. It snapped the roof off the factory my family owned and obliterated every landmark I'd known. A series of other freakish tornadoes touched down in surrounding counties and were as equally destructive. My family members were physically unharmed, but we were shaken to the core, as was the entire town. I went back to college, but I couldn't figure out what to do next. I was haunted by the destruction I'd witnessed and by a combination of feelings: guilt, anger, and longing.

This devastation of my hometown played into a decision I made after I graduated to work with my father in the family business. He told me he wanted to retire, and if I came to work for him, I could take over some of his duties as plant manager. He said he was ready for the change. Mark and my other brother were already part of the business, so I made the decision to join the ranks. I had no other clear path at the time, and I felt a desire to help my town get back on its feet.

I loved working in the plant and with the guys on the plant floor, with whom I had a good connection. I think I was a decent manager and wanted to find a way to update the equipment as well as our relationship with the workers. But in truth, my father would have none of it. It didn't take long before he was sabotaging any changes I wanted to make to move the business forward. It became obvious that he and I were going to lock horns every step of the way, and we did.

Though it was a mistake to work with my father, at least I was earning money—much more than I needed to spend. I had very little sense of what to do with the money, though. I had a broker, but I didn't know and didn't care how any of it worked or how he invested my money. I just kept saving money because I thought it was a good idea, not because I had any kind of plan.

I was making money, but I wasn't leading what I'd call a happy life. It was during this time that an idea entered my brain like a bolt out of the blue. I was twenty-eight years old when it suddenly hit me that I would make a really good pastor or priest. It was a bizarre thought, seeing as I hadn't stepped foot inside a church in more than ten years, and frankly, the thought weirded me out. I had been raised Roman Catholic and, early in my life, felt quite alienated from the church by virtue of being embodied female. My experience in the church in that era was that, by definition, females were "damaged goods." For instance, I had wanted to be an altar server when I was eight years old and was told it was impossible because I was female. In other words, I wasn't good enough. That deep, spiritual woundedness stayed with me. I continued to go to church when I was growing up, mostly because it was required of me, but when I was eighteen and went to college, I left the institutional church behind.

Or so I thought. In hindsight, I didn't completely abandon it. Despite the terrible wounding by the church, it still formed me in many positive ways. I can see now I was following a meandering spiritual path looking for something—a place where I felt welcome, a place of home. This is a theme that permeates much of my life, like it does for many people. This longing was guiding me, though I didn't see it at the time. I believe this bizarre idea that popped in my head was part of that guiding.

This is further illustrated by some decisions I had made in college. I started out as a vocal performance major, but in the first semester, I developed nodes on my larynx. No doubt this had something to do with the fact that I had been a drum major in high school, which required a lot of yelling. By the second semester of my freshman year, I was starting to realize that building a career on a damaged instrument didn't make sense, but I had no idea what else I might do. I was helped in my decision by a fluke role I got, through a little bit of larceny on my part, in a light opera version of "Twelfth Night." Unfortunately, it wasn't singing; it was dancing. Even though I am not a dancer, I ended up in a hoop skirt, learning to promenade and skip across the stage. But I wanted to do it because I thought, "Okay, whatever—at least I'm one step closer to opera."

The singers for this opera were paid professionals, and they were incredible. I remember vividly listening with amazement to these singers up close, especially the male lead tenor. On opening night, we were all standing backstage, excited for the curtain to go up. The dancers were to go out first and the singers would follow. As I stood backstage in my ribbon-bestrewn hoopskirt, feathery headpiece, and caked-on mascara, I realized I was standing next to the lead singer. I couldn't help myself and gushed something like, "I think you have an amazing voice, and I appreciate so much your work," implying, "It must be great to be you." I'll never forget how he looked at me when he answered in a flat, depressed way, "Well, it's really all I know how to do." And in that instant, a curtain fell for me. I thought, "Wow. Well that's not all I know how to do. Hey, I can even dance in a hoop skirt! I'm not going to struggle with this decision anymore—this is my sign that it's time to move on to something else."

I changed to political science, and as part of the coursework, I took a few political philosophy classes and loved them. I was reading Plato and Rousseau and various other philosophers and realized it all fit onto a theological framework. These philosophers presupposed an understanding of the nature of God, or the divine, or whatever you want to call it, and it fascinated me. By the time I graduated, I was thinking, "I sure wish I had studied more of that."

Fast forward to the spiritual bolt of lightning I had while driving down the road, imagining myself as a priest or pastor. The only problem was how much I hated the institutional church. It didn't make any sense. I kept trying to push the idea away, but it would resurface. I saw an advertisement in the newspaper that the local Catholic college was providing a new curriculum for lay people—sort of a lay theological institute. I thought, "I really should think about that," and went so far as to get some information from the nun leading the course, but then didn't follow through. Many months passed, and work at the family business grew steadily more unsatisfying. My father and I continued to butt heads. As I drove to work one day, I sighed to myself. "I really should get back in touch with the nun in that program I looked at."

I walked into the office and the phone rang. The receptionist buzzed through and said, "There's a nun on the phone for you." It was her.

Before she could tell me why she was calling, I said, "Wait, I have to tell you that just this morning I was driving into work, and I was thinking that I should call you!"

She responded easily. "Oh, I know. I've been thinking about you and waiting for you to call. You need to take my course." Needless to say, I took the course and began to do research on what options were out there to pursue my new interest. I applied to a master's program in divinity, was accepted, and resigned from the family business.

I loved divinity school. I literally fell in love with my studies and the whole feeling of the place. I was beginning to find my feet in some ways. One thing that had not changed was my anxiety and confusion around money. I stopped opening my brokerage reports. Dollar signs made me nauseated. By this time, I was married and had a child, and I began to feel more or less constantly worried about money, even as I felt powerless to take hold and control its flow. I had no idea how or if I would ever make a living with my divinity degree. In my classes and among my peers, there was a lot of talk of privilege and preferential options for the poor, the gospel message, and contemplative prayer. I loved it all. The development of my spirituality at this point only reinforced my distrust of and general alienation from business, money, and wealth.

My issues with money no doubt played into the decision I made next, but of course, it was much more complicated than that. During my time in divinity school, I would get regular calls from my father. He would talk about the business and the changes that needed to happen so he could retire. Always the skilled puppet master, my father successfully played all of his children, and I fell for it when he said he was ready for real change in the business. He said he was supporting my brother Mark, who had hired a consultant to help work through some of the business changes that needed to happen. I was invited to come back and be the change agent—to help execute the new plan—and I would be given the support necessary to make this happen. I was an idiot to believe him, but old habits die hard. I felt I had an obligation to do this in order to keep up any relationship with my family. Weeping, I withdrew from school and returned to the business.

It didn't take long for me to realize my mistake. In the end, my father, fearing transition and his imminent displacement, blew up any chance at real change. For me, that tore it. Once again feeling deeply betrayed and this time even used by my father, I said I wanted to sever from the business completely and asked to be bought out. The family agreed.

Fresh off the defeat and alienation I had suffered from the family business and no longer pursuing my divinity degree, I was easily sucked into a venture that came next. I suppose I wanted to prove myself and show my family I could be a success without them, so I sunk almost all the money I had gotten from the buy-out into an innovative, new ergonomic-chair design. The chair itself was fantastic, and the whole idea of "ergonomics" was pretty new in 1993. However, the people I surrounded myself with, including the inventor, were not so great. I learned a very expensive lesson that a great idea is *not* all that is needed to be successful in business. Suffice it to say that I ended up losing all the money, helped my brother Mark and some others also lose money, sabotaged a couple of friendships, and learned one of the most valuable lessons of my life: I could lose all that money and still be alive and basically okay.

A former professor at divinity school convinced me to come back and finish. I didn't know what else to do, so I went. Many positive changes occurred there, including my orientation to the contemplative path separate from the institutional church. I embraced the idea of spiritual practice and began practicing meditation and yoga. These practices strengthened me spiritually, but the messiness of my life persisted. My first marriage ended, and a new relationship began. I adopted children and struggled through and paid dearly the court system as my new partner disentangled from a mentally ill former spouse. The stress showed up for me in a series of physical problems, but I managed to complete my coursework, even though I had no idea what I would do next.

Money was part of the mess too. Isn't it always? I still had a little money left in my investments, but it was definitely waning. I was anxious about money but mostly in denial. I would oscillate between feeling rich and feeling impoverished. It was haunting me, but I had absolutely no idea how to speak of it or with whom I could discuss it.

All along this journey I was stumbling. I would have moments of clarity, only to come across a roadblock that would stymie me. So many times I would find myself up against a wall with no visible way forward. I would say to myself, "Here I am again, standing at the door, and there's no knob to turn." I would stand at the wall, which seemed impenetrable, then miraculously I would fall through, and a path would appear. That's been my experience over and over in life—a sense that something is leading me. It was at this point in my life that I heard the message I mentioned in the introduction of this book, "Get up and deal with your money."

Today, when I look back on my life, I see I was on a spiritual path, though it usually wasn't clear to me at the time. I actually believe this is true for all of us. We're all on a spiritual path, whether we choose to recognize it or not. And I'd say that money has been on that path too—leading the way for some, hanging around the shadows for others, or being dragged behind like a lead weight. It's critical to look back at the path on which we've been traveling—money and all—and be honest and compassionate with ourselves about what the path included. Only by taking stock of the past can we move on in a healthy way to the present and the future. Examining my past this way was an important step for my own spiritual journey. There were several components to that examination, but one helpful step was becoming a Certified Money Coach (CMC)® through the Money Coaching Institute with Deborah Price.[1] During that process I completed several helpful exercises, though it's not necessary to complete the training to benefit from the exercises. The three sections below, "Money Memories," "Money and Your Family of Origin," and "Money Energies," including the practice exercises in those sections—though adapted by me—come from Deborah's book *Money Magic: Unleashing Your True Potential for Prosperity and Fulfillment*[2] and are used with her permission.

Money Memories

We all have a story, and—more specifically—we all have a story in relationship to money. Some may feel attached to these stories and want to maintain a particular script. Some may feel ashamed or embarrassed by their histories and feel uncomfortable sharing them. Whatever your personal experience and history around money, telling your story is essential in order to witness it objectively and consciously. We must be willing to observe how we have developed and manifested certain beliefs and behaviors in our history and in relationship with money. We must do this, not with judgment or fear, but with clear-eyed honesty, though this is not an easy task. The point is not to criticize anyone—ourselves or those who parented us—but to raise our consciousness so we know what we're dealing with and, to some extent, why. Many people have looked back at their lives and examined their childhood and young adult memories and patterns to help them understand their situation in the present, but in my experience, it is unusual to do this through the lens of money.

I consider my earliest memory involving money to be the day my beloved nanny Ann suddenly disappeared when I was four years old, as I described in chapter 1. For all intents and purposes, she had been my mother, but one day I woke up, and she was just not there. When I asked my mother where Ann was, I was told only that she was not coming back because my father had "fired" her. I had no idea what that meant, but I was devastated. I never got a chance to say goodbye. Of course, I didn't understand the connection between this memory and money until I was older. As Ann's employer, my father had power over whether she stayed in my life or left. Ultimately, his money created my relationship with her, dictated its evolution, and dissolved it, along with my confidence in that bond—a powerful message.

I believe this early event in my life laid the groundwork for a constant fear of abandonment and betrayal. As an adult, when I looked back at that memory through the lens of money, I saw how money kindled those fears of abandonment and betrayal. It reinforced an idea that I must be on one particular side of that power play in order to avoid future betrayals. Other memories when viewed through this lens also helped me see how I became the person I am today. When I sat down and wrote out these memories—my father literally dropping my "net worth" on me and walking away, the class differences I witnessed in my home-town, the way my parents used money in their own lives for good and as manipulation—patterns and new understandings were revealed about myself. Once I was aware of these, I could begin the work of moving beyond them to a deeper level.

Another example of an early money memory comes from a friend. She remembers her mother giving her a nickel to put in the church collection plate each Sunday. Even though she was only three or four at the time, she remembers vividly the image of her mother reaching into her pocketbook and handing her the shiny nickel, watching the wooden ring of the collection plate with its crushed-velvet lining move toward her, and feeling the coin drop into the plate. Infused in that memory is a hushed reverence and sense of the holy around money, as well as an emphasis on giving and gratitude. As you can imagine, this vivid memory is reflected in many aspects of my friend's dealings with money and her own spiritual journey.

PRACTICE:
Track Your Money Memories

Start by setting aside some quiet time to think about your past. This exploration should take some time and probably more than one session. Be sure to give yourself plenty of time. Have with you a way to write down your memories. When you're ready, close your eyes and scan your memories from early childhood. Start with the first money memory you can recall. Write it down, including how old you were and a brief accounting of the experience that occurred (a few sentences will suffice). It's not necessary to go into great detail about the memory; rather, just state the memory, your age at the time, and any feelings you recall having around the experience. If you have trouble coming up with an early memory, just write down your earliest money memory, whenever it is, and more may follow.

Now, with your first money memory as the starting point, continue to write your money memories chronologically from this point forward up until present day. Include any significant memories you can recall, including those pertaining to your parents, grandparents, or other family members. Be sure to include how these experiences affected you and your feelings associated with each memory. Write down a memory for each year, as much as you're able, because placing yourself in the time period helps memories surface.

When you finish this practice, you will probably have several pages of memories. This outcome will be your financial autobiography. Going through this practice can be eye-opening and can act as a base to some of the other practices mentioned in this book. Looking back at your journey so far can influence where you go next.

Money and Your Family of Origin

I have a client, I'll call him Ray, who grew up in a church missionary household. His religious parents served in several countries throughout Africa during his youth, and the family lived quite modestly within the communities they served. Since the family was completely dependent on the church and had very little money of their own, the parents allowed no extravagance, though they did know their basic needs would always be met. They were immersed in the communities they served, but were also "outsiders" in a sense—neither all in nor all out. As an adult, Ray took a more traditional, middle-class job in the United States and was successful at supporting himself. But his ambivalence about money was extreme. On the one hand, he had felt deprived as a child, desiring little "extras" he never got. So as an adult he longed for these extras and would sometimes purchase them. But as soon as he did, the voices of his parents came into his head, and the guilt set in. The shine dulled on the things he thought he had wanted, leaving him unable to enjoy them. At the same time, he was almost excessively generous, giving away money and gifts whenever he could, but unable to enjoy that as well. When it came to money, his parents' voices, and the voices of the church, were eating him up.

The influence our parents and other important figures in our lives have on our relationships with money cannot be overemphasized. Perhaps this influence stands out more strongly in one family member than another. If a family follows traditional roles, the father may be "in charge" of the finances, while the mother is passive. Or it may be the other way around. There may be conflict over money if both parents differ on how to handle it. Opposites do attract sometimes, with one spouse hoping the other will fill in his or her missing gaps or "fix" their own problems. We all know people in this kind of push-pull relationship, for instance the wife who says she's frugal because her spouse is such a spender, or the person who married someone because she was such a free spirit and fun, while he didn't know how to have fun. But they never talk about any of these issues and suddenly find themselves circling the drain. On the other hand, there are families where both parents are on the same page about finances, but another family member—a grandparent or sibling perhaps—throws a wrench into the well-oiled machinery. Some families use money to cover up traumatic dysfunctions like addiction and mental problems. Each family is unique, but they all have their money patterns and difficulties, large or small.

I've talked about my own parents and their relationships and habits around money. As I look back at how I was brought up, I see a lot of both of my parents in myself: Like my mother, I can be generous and open in the wider community but have a harder time on an individual level. Like my father, I want to be a good provider, but I can feel anxious if I sense I'm not "in control." I have other attributes that are not like my parents, but it's been eye-opening to recognize the helpful and not-so-helpful ones I've inherited from them.

This influence includes our parents' individual styles, but it's larger than that too, including the broader "family culture" around money. (Think of my family's fusion of the business and the family.) If wealth and the accumulation of it is part of a family's culture, this is likely to last for generations. A 2015 study found that children raised in wealthy families turned out wealthy, whether they were biological children or adopted. Although this study didn't try to pinpoint exactly what in the environment was creating this trend, they found it was not related entirely to wealth being passed on from one generation to the other. Something about the larger culture around the family and money—savings patterns, aversion to debt, feelings about wealth or the lack of it, patterns around charity and financial giving, and so on—played an important role in whether the children of wealthy people were also wealthy.[3]

But genetics *can* play a part. The new and fascinating study of behavioral epigenetics is showing that traumatic experiences in our recent ancestors' past can leave molecular scars on our DNA. In other words, our ancestors' experiences can affect our own brains and, therefore, our own experiences. Studies show that traumas experienced in one generation, such as the Jews during the Holocaust or children who have been abused, can show up as inherited psychological and behavioral tendencies in future generations, even if the specific memories are forgotten.[4] I see this played out in my own family. The trauma of my grandfather and his son falling out over money in the 1950s and the ensuing court case and severed relationships continues to permeate the family culture around money to this day. An excavation of my own family's stories, tendencies, and habits around money helped me become more aware of this underlying darkness permeating the family dynamic and where it may—in part—have originated. My friend Ray, mentioned at the beginning of this section, also found help by looking at his family of origin through the lens of money—his parents as well as the larger structure of the church to which the family was inextricably tied. Acknowledgment of such elements is the first step in changing them and starting down a different path.

PRACTICE:
The Parent Mirror

This exercise is designed to help you explore the qualities, characteristics, and energy you experienced in each of your parents (or parent, if you had only one;

or guardian, if you were not raised by a parent). It's important not to censor this information. Instead, allow yourself to be completely honest about your feelings and experiences. You'll receive the best results by completing this exercise in a stream of consciousness manner.

Begin by closing your eyes and visualizing your parents one at a time, starting with whoever appears first. Once you have formed a clear image of your first parent, make a list of words that describe the qualities, characteristics, and energy that you attribute to this parent, especially in regard to money. Use descriptive adjectives or very short phrases. Allow the words that describe this parent to come from your memory without analyzing them, until you feel complete and have nothing more to add to your list. Then repeat this process for your other parent, unless you had only one. If you have a significant body of experiences and money memories related to any other significant relatives, particularly grandparents, complete this same process for them as well.

Once you have completed these lists, you'll ask yourself a series of questions. Which parent do I most resemble, or mirror? Which aspects of my parents' relationships to money come up in my life? What perceptions do I have about my parents in regard to money? Which aspects do I openly embrace and which do I deny? Are there aspects of my parents' behavior I have completely rebelled against and has this rebellion been beneficial? What feelings came up for me while I was doing this exercise? Did I notice any tendencies about myself that I might want to change?

You may or may not be happy with what comes up in this exercise. You might realize you have some tendencies you wish you didn't. That's okay. Let the judgment go. As I've said before, awareness of these trends and past patterns is the first step to a new path.

Money Types or Energies

Once we've taken a closer look at our past through the lens of money, we can begin to look at the person we are today in a more honest and realistic way. Even so, some of our current tendencies around money may not initially be visible, lurking as they often do in the dark rooms of the unconscious. In *Money Magic*, Deborah Price delineates eight "Money Types" and offers a system for helping people see the archetypal energies or patterns that are strongest in them. I jokingly refer to this as "Jung meets the Enneagram," as the psychologist Carl Jung advanced the concept of psychological archetypes and the Enneagram is a typology of personality types. In her training classes, Deborah says, "This system helps people see not 'who they are' but 'where they are,' so they can become aware of and change unconscious behaviors around money."

People I work with often find such categories helpful, so I introduce them to Deborah's Money Types so they can see where they fit in. (You can fill out Deborah's "Money Type Quiz" for free on her website, http://moneycoachinginstitute. com/understanding-money-types/.) However, I caution that such designations are simply tools for awareness; they are not written in stone, and they can and will morph over time. Most of us have elements of all the categories within us, and each type has positive and negative elements. There is no one type that represents the correct way to relate to money—some are more positive, some fairly destructive, some mixed. This is not a reified typology, such as the astrological signs (as in, you're either a Pisces, or you're not), so it's not helpful to assume you fit snuggly in one or two categories and leave it at that. That's the danger of such a system—it's easy to assume you're a certain type and begin to conform reality to it. Instead, you want to use these descriptors as tools to notice what is dominant in you at any particular moment in time. Then use your newfound acknowledgment to encourage those patterns you want to strengthen, and transform those that seem to be unhealthy and blocking your way.

Because of my hesitation with typologies, I prefer to use the term *Money Energies*, instead of Deborah's term *Money Types*. *Energies*, in my opinion, speaks to the somewhat fluid nature of these patterns and tendencies, whereas Deborah sees them as more distinct behaviors. In this section, I use the term *Money Energies* and have modified the ideas some-what, but the concepts on which they are based are Deborah's "Money Types."

Just to add another layer to this discussion, I've added other illustrations of "Money Energies" beyond the traditional Jungian archetypes. The names in parenthesis are taken from the 1946 classic film *It's a Wonderful Life*. I can't remember when I first saw this film. I was probably in my teens, but I have a vague sense that I didn't really understand it the first time I saw it. When I hit adulthood, which for me really got going after I had children, I began to watch it every holiday season. As my children grew older, I would invite (actually, somewhat insist!) that they watch it with me. Now it is a family tradition, albeit a mixed one. By that I mean, as my kids have grown older, they say that every year they watch it the plotline grows darker. I agree. In truth, the film is not all that heartwarming, though it seemingly ends well. What I love about it, however, is that it is a tale of two very different views of money, business, and capitalism, and I think those competing visions are alive and well today in business and most especially in politics.

I'm sure I am also drawn to this movie because it portrays a family business and the desire of the founder's kids to get out of their small town and see the world. (Sound familiar?) George Bailey Sr. is a kind, loving man who founds the Bailey Building and Loan, the kind of banking establishment that demands a sense of community to be successful. It was designed, first and foremost, to make home ownership available to the "common man" by leveraging the savings of the community to help one another achieve the American dream. This building and loan doesn't maximize profit. It has no shareholders but the savers who put their money in this little institution and allow it to be lent to their fellow townspeople, trusting they will be paid back with a reasonable amount of interest. The folks who run it are decidedly middle class and committed to their community and to giving folks options beyond the traditional banking channel for home loans.

By contrast, the movie's villain, Mr. Potter, is the ultimate rapacious capitalist who cares only for his own bottom line— having no family or children or friends of his own. He is an angry, frustrated older man who seems bent on the economic ruin of others, especially the Bailey Building and Loan, with whom he must compete. He holds a controlling interest in the local bank, and a board seat at the building and loan. And he is forever pressuring George Sr. to be more aggressive in terms of maximizing profit. He is also basically a slumlord, so the building and loan's mission to help folks get out of nasty rental properties and into their own homes—especially immigrants—cuts into Potter's business.

The film treats us to a magical portrayal of the little town, Bedford Falls, had George Jr. not kept the building and loan alive after the sudden death of his father and instead followed his own wanderlust out of town. The climax occurs when, on Christmas Eve, money comes up missing from the building and loan (viewers see it has basically been stolen by Mr. Potter), and George Jr. recognizes he is "worth more dead than alive" and decides to commit suicide. He is saved by his guardian angel, Clarence Odbody, who decides the best way to turn George's feelings around is to show him life in his town had he never been born. We get a glimpse of "Pottersville" without George Jr. and the building and loan, and find a dystopian version of a small town that is primarily one of bars, dance halls, and all manner of unsavory desolation devoid of community, care, and tidy middle-class homes. People are angry and desperate.

But mercifully, George Jr. stays in Bedford Falls and discovers he does have a "wonderful life" after all. The movie ends with the unmistakable understanding that George's role in the community, leading the building and loan, was essential to the thriving of Bedford Falls. We're left unclear as to what ultimately happens to Potter, though one might look at our current sociopolitical situation and conclude that the Potters of the world and their attitudes and influence have certainly not waned.

What follows below is an outline of these archetypes and their corresponding character from the movie. I highly recommend you watch it through the lens of these Money Energies.

The Innocent (Uncle Billy)

Sandy is a perky woman with big, blue eyes and a warm smile. She works as a dental hygienist and enjoys being mother to her two children. What she doesn't enjoy is thinking about money—someone else has always handled that for her. She never learned about finances growing up because her father gave her an allowance and paid her bills, and that was fine with her. She married young, and her husband, Peter, handled the money. The money she makes from work is deposited directly into her checking account. She writes checks and uses credit cards but doesn't pay much attention to the statements—her husband always let her know if there was an issue. Recently, her husband left her after fifteen years of marriage. She was devastated and angry, but deep down, she hoped he would come to his senses and come back. For one thing, she was afraid she couldn't make it on her own. Reluctantly, she moved from part-time work to full time and now receives alimony. She has no idea if she has enough money to live on, but she's afraid she doesn't. So she hired an accountant to do her taxes and a financial planner. She told the planner, "Please, you just tell me what to do—I hate thinking about this stuff."

Sandy has a lot of tendencies of the Innocent. Her approach to money is like the ostrich with its head in the sand. People like Sandy tend to be happy-go-lucky on the outside, but a little fearful and anxious on the inside. Their basic thought is, "I don't want to deal with this and I wish it would go away." Or, "Somebody I love and trust should take care of this for me." This kind of energy seeks security, but is indecisive. They want others to help them so they will feel "safe," but there's often an underlying fear that whoever is helping them will abandon them. They are not empowered themselves.

People who want to move away from their negative Innocent energies need to begin to do what they least want to do; namely, engage more directly with their money: look at their statements, balance their checkbooks, read articles online, ask questions about what they're signing. In other words, they need to get help in understanding their finances, rather than hoping it will go away or someone else will handle it. This doesn't have to mean becoming a financial wizard, but some ownership of this aspect of their life will go a long way.

Uncle Billy in *It's a Wonderful Life* has Innocent energies. He's happy and funny on the surface, but inside he's fearful and anxious. He's dependent on George Sr. and then George Jr. for his job, even though he's fairly unskilled and scatter-brained—always tying a string around his finger to remember something he's forgotten. In the dystopian view of Bedford Falls—when we are allowed to see the town if George Jr. had never been born—we're told that Uncle Billy has "gone insane" after the building and loan went out of business. He is also the character that loses the bank deposit causing the building and loan to possibly fail, but George Jr. takes responsibility for his error to keep Billy from going to jail. For Uncle Billy, the Innocent, when problems arise, he's nonconfrontational but worried, turning to alcohol to make his problems go away.

The Victim (Pottersville's Ma Bailey)

Frank owns a small construction company with several employees. His business has had its ups and downs, but he always made a decent living, at least up until the latest recession. Then things got rough and he had to lay off two employees. He greatly resents this and blames the current political administration, which he declares loudly and often on social media. Recently, a subcontractor he's worked with for years made a small mistake that cost Frank several hundred dollars. Despite the positive, longtime working relationship they had in the past, Frank refused to acknowledge that it was a one-time mistake and told the subcontractor, "I always knew you were going to screw me one of these days," and ended the relationship. He imagines the early years of his business as the glory days but thinks the world has always been out to get him—that's why he doesn't make more money. Despite his complaints about the economy and his business, Frank doesn't look realistically at his finances. He bought a new truck last month, telling himself he needed it to help the business get back on its feet. On a deeper level he was thinking, "What the hell. This world is never going to let me be a success. I might as well get my piece of the pie while I can."

This is Victim energy, which is—I'm sorry to say—abroad in the land. And I don't just mean on an individual level. There are whole societal networks built around exploiting Victim energy. One of the fundamental ways politicians get elected these days is to promise to "bring back the good old days" by making things "great again." And why are they not great now, one might ask? The Victim mentality will assure you that it has nothing to do with *you*—it is someone else's fault. And that someone else is often a person of color, or a person who is a new American, or a person who is just not like you. "This is all somebody else's fault. If only those _____ wouldn't come to this country, we'd be okay. Our politicians only look out for themselves while they're supposed to be rescuing us. Why isn't anybody saving me?" In fact, whole news outlets are built on selling this idea.

But the news networks and the politicians are only successful because it rings the bell of the Victim energy inside us. And most of us have at least a little of this lurking around in our psyches. It is made even trickier because there are people who are legitimately being victimized, and I don't want to discredit that. Many people are dealing with real financial disasters brought on through no fault of their own. Sometimes the factory closes up shop, taking the jobs they once provided to another part of the United States or another country, leaving few other options for people in the area. Little wonder some become angry and bitter and look for someone to blame, even if those they are blaming have nothing to do with what happened to them. This is the tragedy: the way this Victim energy is used as a tool of manipulation by others to build themselves up and consolidate their own power.

Victim energy is not always based in reality, and digging down to the truth can be difficult. The internal story that is keeping the person trapped may be a past reality that the person has never been able to move beyond. It's the voice in us that says, "It doesn't matter what I do. I won't get ahead or be financially stable—I might as well do what I want." Or, "I've had bad luck. I'm entitled to this." It can lead to financial irresponsibility or a belief that we're entitled to be rescued. Unfortunately, this kind of energy can feed on itself and draw further negativity toward it. If someone who is caught in this Victim energy doesn't trust you, they'll be looking for betrayal—something to pounce on to prove they have been right about you or whoever or whatever groups they seek to blame.

Those wanting to let go of this energy will need to start recognizing what they themselves are responsible for in their financial situation, and begin to make changes. For many, what underlies Victim energy is anger toward themselves that comes out as anger toward others. By this, I mean that people who get caught here are often secretly self-loathing. Deep down, they blame themselves for their victimization, but they cannot face the powerlessness this implies in their life. In their desperation, they externalize their own self-hatred and cast that blame onto others rather than face it. Thus, it seems the first most difficult task for those caught in Victim energy is to *forgive themselves* for past behaviors so they can move on. They must also strive to forgive those who have truly victimized them in the past. This must start with an understanding of what actually happened. Looking at these wounds at a deep, systemic level requires more than a cursory look—it requires patience and discipline. It's often easier to believe whatever story you're being told than to look deeper into the situation to figure out what is actually going on around you.

We live in an era of diabolical propaganda coming at us from every direction. Getting to the truth is a full-time spiritual practice. One tip: If the answer is easy or conveniently suggests that someone else is fully to blame, you are likely not at the truth. The truth is often quite complicated, and in our current state of affairs, we tend to favor sound bites.

At the same time, forgiveness is not the same as putting oneself in a position to be victimized again. It's simply trying to let go of the things that hook us into believing we are the Victim. Hanging on to old resentments is like taking poison in order to harm someone else. We only harm ourselves.

Ma Bailey in *It's a Wonderful Life*—that is, Ma from the dystopian reality of Pottersville—is suspicious, distrustful, and bitter. When George comes to her house looking for help and mentions her brother, Uncle Billy, she turns him away, suspecting he's trying to take advantage of her. "I don't take in strangers," she says with an acid edge in her voice. Then she tells George he belongs in the "insane asylum" just like Billy and slams the door in his face. Things have gone bad for Ma Bailey, and we see it in her posture, her dark brooding stare, and her anger. We don't know from the movie all the things that happened to Ma Bailey that caused this dramatic change in her personality, but the chief culprit was certainly the triumph of Potter over the hope that the building and loan promised. She is a victim indeed, now having to take in boarders to make ends meet. At the same time, she has not found a way to overcome her extreme resentfulness at the cards life has dealt her.

The Warrior (Sam Wainwright)

Caroline gets things done, and she does them with skill and determination. She was a top student in law school and set herself a goal of becoming partner in seven years. She made it in six. In addition to being a good lawyer, Caroline understands the finance world and likes to do her own investing. Her wife is not as successful financially as Caroline and prefers not to think about the finances. That's okay with Caroline because she likes the idea of being the provider for her family and is a generous caretaker. She does tend to work too much, and when not working, she has a hard time relaxing. While at home with the family watching a movie, she can't seem to stay off her phone, checking email or the latest stock quotes. She finds a kind of addictive satisfaction in staying on top of the work, even though it sometimes annoys those who are close to her. Still, it's made her financially successful.

We all know people like Caroline, or perhaps we are like her—someone with a lot of entrepreneurial initiative. For them, dealing with money is fun, and some are very good at it. They rely on their own instincts and are generally on target. The Warrior energy is focused, decisive, and gets things completed. My father is a great example. The caveat is that people with strong Warrior energies can get into the "sport" of it and forget it's related to anything meaningful in their lives. Dealing with money becomes the thing itself. I have known people who have made lots of money in life, then retired and were miserable. They didn't know what to do with themselves because making money was all they knew how to do. They were caught in the money-making habit and didn't want to give up the power and sheer fun it gave them.

The goal for people who want to change the negative parts of this energy is to look at what's truly important and begin focusing on that. What is it you're actually making money for? Who do you want to protect and care for? How do you balance making money to do this and enjoy the life and security that money gives you? It's also helpful to look at those who cause conflict in our lives as an opportunity for growth and change rather than an adversary to be "beaten" at all costs.

Sam Wainwright captures this in *It's a Wonderful Life*. Sam is the friend of Mary and George who gets in on the ground floor of the plastics industry in the 1920s and '30s, becoming wealthy and successful. In the movie, he is portrayed as someone who inherited the opportunity, as it is his father who helps him get into business, but who also understands the business world and is blithely unconflicted about making tons of money! He is somewhat goofy and materialistic, but also seems full of a joy de vivre. So his good business sense is balanced by a sense of joy and optimism. He enacts a kind of generative capitalism that looks to hire more people, grow more jobs, and so on. Not at all the kind of stingy, angry view we see portrayed by Potter. Sam is also deeply generous. Early on in his career, Sam encourages George and Mary to buy stock in his father's plastic business, which would have been a financial boon if they had taken him up on it. And when George and the building and loan are in trouble after Uncle Billy has misplaced the bank deposit, it is Sam—off in Europe at the time—who cables to say he has instructed his office to wire him up to $25,000—an enormous sum in 1945!

The Martyr (George Bailey Jr.)

Lester has been the minister at the same two-hundred-member church for twelve years. Most of the members of his congregation think the world of him, and why wouldn't they? In addition to delivering a pretty good sermon, he's always there when anyone is in the hospital or needs to speak with him about something personal. Plus, he's in charge of the food drive and the clothing drive and the youth-group bake sale and the church's volunteer evening at the soup kitchen. He's that kind of guy, putting everyone else first—that's his calling, right? But secretly, underneath that clerical collar, he often feels let down and resentful. And it's not just his work. Lester feels the same way about his money. He'd give most people the shirt off his back, and—in fact—he's loaned (or given) his friend Tom several thousand dollars over the past ten years. Tom has had some problems, and Lester claims to be sympathetic. But secretly he also believes a lot of those problems were Tom's own fault. Of course, he doesn't say that to Tom. He bails him out, while inside he's seething, fantasizing about what he would say to him if he weren't such a "good person." Interestingly, Lester's congregation has grown to take on this kind of energy as well, though Lester's not aware of it. The organization presents itself as a serving congregation—and it is. But there's an underlying resentfulness, especially when it comes to spending money, and a judgmental edge to their giving.

Like with all the Money Energies, Martyr energy can be found in most of us to some extent or another. We all know people or organizations with a high dose of it: resentful, self-sacrificing, long-suffering. On the outside they may be smiling, but inside they're saying to themselves, "If I have to take one more casserole to some needy family I'm going to choke—or better yet—choke them!" They are often perfectionists, expecting a lot from themselves and others and living with disappointment. There is certainly nothing wrong with caring for others, or giving of our time, energy, and money. We want to have that energy. The problem comes when the energy is used to rescue others while taking away their opportunity to help themselves, or when the giving comes at the expense of the giver. That's why the flight attendant on the airplane always tells us to cover our own mouths with the oxygen mask first before helping others with theirs. You can't lend a hand to someone else until you first have solid footing yourself.

People trying to change their Martyr energy need to focus on taking better care of themselves first, and not manipulating others into doing it for them. Similarly, they need to look at the underlying reasons for their caretaking and where the motivation is coming from. For many who have Martyr energy showing up, one of the underlying reasons is that they only feel "good" if they have done something for someone else. They are not "enough" just as they are. Paradoxically, as they help others, they are certainly getting something from the bargain—a sense of self-worth—but one that comes at the cost of their own self-care. As a consequence, they project onto others their need to be needed, and certainly there are others out there whose own dominant Money Energies are only too happy to play along. Letting go of the expectation that others should be grateful for your help is key here. Healthy giving is done with an open hand and an open heart. Once the heart begins to close, it's a sign that there are imbalances afoot.

It's a Wonderful Life protagonist George Bailey Jr. suffers from some serious Martyr leanings. He stays home to help his father take care of the building and loan and gives his college money to his brother, so he can go instead. He dreams of building bridges and traveling, but when his father dies, he gives up his dreams to keep the business going. He also gives up his honeymoon, which was set to begin on Black Monday 1929. Instead, he and his wife Mary give all their travel money to those wanting to make a withdrawal that day. Even when Uncle Billy loses $8,000, George yells at him, "Somebody's going to jail, and it's not going to be me," but in the end, he claims it was his own fault. At the same time, he resents it all, feeling guilty and self-sacrificing about it, and doesn't see the joy in his life. In fact, his desperation and self-loathing lead him to contemplate suicide. Of course, Mr. Potter is right there to encourage him. As George is forced to go to Potter for a last-minute loan to replace the lost bank deposits, Potter sneeringly asks him if he has any collateral of any kind to back the loan he is requesting. George replies that he owns "no securities, no stocks, no bonds," but does have five hundred dollars' equity in a life insurance policy. Potter, smelling the opportunity to push his rival over the edge replies, "Well, George, it seems you're worth more dead than alive." George, now habituated to doing what must be done regardless of the cost to himself, and increasingly angry and dark at the prospect, takes the bait and the anger turns inward. He heads to the nearest bridge to jump, but is saved by angelic intervention and an extraordinary opportunity to see how the world would look if he hadn't been born. To someone fully in the grip of Martyr energy, this might seem like vindication. After all, his self-sacrifice is rewarded in the end when he is given the gift of a vision showing him how much his sacrifice has meant. But one would hope that these were not our only choices: self-denial to the point of exhaustion, depression, and suicide, or relinquishing one's destiny, leading to the dissolution of the community.

The Tyrant (Mr. Potter)

There are many people who admire Don and respect him, but because of his Tyrant tendencies, he is not generally thought of as a likable man. Frankly though, he doesn't care. He owns two successful car dealerships, and has amassed a certain amount of wealth, but he doesn't come from a wealthy family. He worked his way up to his current position by making savvy business dealings. His father was an alcoholic, and Don learned early on how to control his environment to avoid his father's abuse. He likes being in control of his business, his employees, his family, and his money. He's also usually in control of his emotions, but occasionally a burst of anger erupts seemingly out of nowhere, making most people wary in his presence. Don genuinely cares about his family, and he's not without generosity. He just shows it through manipulation. He has given donations to his alma mater, his church, and several nonprofit organizations, but usually there are strings attached: programs administered the way he designates, friends added to certain committees, his name on a placard—that sort of thing. His grown children know this tendency well. Don can be generous with them, but he expects certain behaviors in return—otherwise, there will be hell to pay.

People with Tyrant energy use money to control people, events, and circumstances. At its core, this energy springs from deep-rooted fears and can spread easily into anger, almost like an addiction. This energy might have started in a healthy way—perhaps as a kind of Warrior energy—but it has grown wild into a tool for power. A lot of people assume that the wealthy must have a strong dose of this energy; that it's almost a requirement. This has not been my experience. Tyrant energy can be found in people with a little or a lot of money. If money is used to control others, and that control is based in fear and anger, the Tyrant is showing its colors.

Moving out of the realm of the Tyrant is not easy because it tends to be deeply based and rooted in an almost infantile fear of loss of control. Of course, the first step is recognizing these tendencies and where they come from. The goal is to see that there is such a thing as "enough" and not constantly live in fear of not having it. The goal is to replace rage and the need for control with acceptance, true generosity, and forgiveness and compassion for oneself and others.

It's not hard to see who the Tyrant is in *It's a Wonderful Life.* As a somewhat one-dimensional movie character, Mr. Potter fits the model perfectly in his black suit and heavy wooden wheelchair being pushed around by his flunky. He has a lot of money and uses it to get more. With no family, he seems to care about nothing but control over all the businesses in Bedford Falls. In fact, in a scene where he tries to win George Bailey over to his side, he says, "George, I'm an old man, and most people hate me. But I don't like them either, so that makes it all even." He goes on to add that the one thing in town he doesn't own is the Bailey Building and Loan, and for years he's been trying to "get control of it or kill it." Fortunately, George doesn't fall for his manipulations. In the end, Potter is not able to bury the building and loan through fair business competition, so he does what Tyrants around the world continue to do—cheat and steal. Uncle Billy folds the cash deposit in a newspaper, accidently laying it in Potter's lap. Upon realizing his spoils, Potter sets about to take full advantage of the situation. Realizing the building and loan will come up short on its deposits, Potter calls in the bank examiners and swears out a warrant for George's arrest, even as he sits back and holds the cash. He is a truly despicable character, and we're given no inclination in the film that he can be redeemed. One hopes for a different outcome for those of us whose Tyrant energy shows its ugly head now and again and who truly want to change for the sake of themselves and those with whom he or she has a relationship.

The Fool (Clarence Odbody)

Everybody loves Lynette—she's so much fun! She's a free spirit who genuinely doesn't seem to worry about much of anything, a refreshing change for many of her friends. They worry less and feel younger when they're around her. Lynette has held several jobs, but currently works for a landscaping company. She doesn't make a lot of money, but that doesn't keep her from doing the things she wants to do. She likes to travel and figures she'll come up with a way to pay the bills eventually. Amazingly, she often does, when small windfalls fall into her lap. But not always. At times she's had to max out her credit cards or borrow from her friends and family. Most of the time, she pays it back. She's generous and loves to give gifts, even though others sometimes end up paying for them, rather than her. But she's so easygoing and fun that her friends and family have a hard time saying no to her.

Everyone loves the Fool. People with Fool energy are fun and spontaneous. Unlike the Innocent, who may seem optimistic on the outside but inside is anxious, the Fool is genuinely optimistic, inside and out. They also tend to be very generous. They're happy to give you whatever you need, even if it's not theirs to give! What's appealing about this energy is that its motto is "live for today," which has a kind of sweetness and exhilaration to it. The problem is it's not always grounded in reality. People with a lot of this energy are not quite telling themselves the whole story. They're looking for windfalls by taking financial shortcuts and hoping things work out. Sometimes things do turn out well for them because they were willing to take a chance. But sometimes they don't, and that can affect other people. They don't want to look at things realistically or bother to do the math because they might miss out on something. No, that would be a downer.

Those who wish to hold onto the positive aspects of Fool energy, but let go of the negative, need to focus on balance. Living in the moment is good, but not with a complete denial of reality. In fact, the central tenant the Fool must embrace is truth—the truth about themselves and their situation. Being trusting and generous is good, but so is being wise and discerning. It's a balancing act.

In *It's a Wonderful Life*, Clarence Odbody, George Bailey's guardian angel, has a bit of the Fool in him. He exists quite literally outside of the money system, so he's the perfect image of this energy. He's so excited when he's told he'll be returning to earth to help George that at first he just wants to figure out what to wear. He has no clue how difficult it's going to be to convince George that he shouldn't throw away his life. In Nick's bar, Clarence seems oblivious to the harsh reality around him (and to the fact that he has no money) and orders a "flaming rum punch," then changes that to "mulled wine, heavy on the cinnamon and light on the cloves." The rough bartender in the George-less, dystopian Pottersville is not amused and throws him and George out into the snow. Clarence is generous too, jumping into the churning river so George will dive in and rescue him instead of drowning himself. In the end, though he is a bit of a Fool, Clarence's efforts are rewarded with divine wings.

The Creator/Artist (Mary Hatch Bailey)
Teresa is a potter who makes gorgeous dinnerware with a blue-green glaze, as well as exotic sculptures that look a bit like sea creatures. Though it hasn't been easy, she's been able to make a frugal living as an artist by selling her work at festivals and galleries and by supplementing her income with freelance articles she's written on the subject of pottery. She loves the little studio in the back of her house and can easily immerse herself all day in her artwork. But she doesn't much enjoy the business side of things. She does her own marketing and bookkeeping, but only reluctantly, because she knows she has to in order to make a living. She has a hard time figuring out how to price her pieces so they reflect the work she's put into them as well as the reality of the current market. Some people

tell her they're overpriced; some say underpriced. Although she doesn't say it out loud (much), she looks down on people she perceives to have "sold out." On the other hand, some of these people are the ones who have enough money to purchase her pottery. She has a love-hate relationship with money.

The energy of the Creator/Artist is one of spirit and creativity. People with a strong level of this energy tend to be internally motivated and non-materialistic. The problem is that they like the freedom that money brings, but don't want to be "sullied" by the material world. They may feel that because they are spiritual beings, they should not have to deal with money. Many people with this kind of energy live happily with very little money, but there are others with a lot of Creator/Artist energy who have plenty of money. The issue is not the amount of money they have, but the fear that they're not being true to themselves and the belief that money is somehow tainting them. Trying to work and live with this belief can undermine the Creator/Artist's work in the world and their possible contributions, not to mention their financial success.

People who want to move beyond the negative aspects of this energy need to reconnect with the incarnational aspects of money. The task is to work toward integration of the spiritual and material world and embrace the dual nature of their path. A hallmark of many of the world's great religions is the understanding that the material and the physical are indeed *not* separate. The deep penetration of the spiritual into the material is one of the central tenants of Christianity in particular, hence the "scandal" of the divine taking human form and dwelling among us. Even so, many forms of Christianity continue to have difficulty with this teaching. For the Creator/Artist energy, the suspicion around materiality—especially as expressed through the monetary system—is very strong. While there are certainly understandable reasons for this, overcoming it and learning to close the "split" is part of a spiritual practice that strives for balance in all things.

The one character in *It's a Wonderful Life* who most approximates this energy is George's wife, Mary, though it's not a perfect fit. Like the Creator/Artist, she is not at all materialistic. At the beginning of the movie, she eschews the advances of Sam Wainwright, the wealthy inheritor and entrepreneur, in favor of her real love for George. She doesn't mind living in a drafty, leaky house, as long as she can pursue her joys: raising her family and helping others. She offers up their honeymoon money to save the building and loan during the bank run of 1929, and then creatively turns that same drafty house into a honeymoon hotel. She embraces the balance between creativity and prosperity, saying to the Martini family when they move into their new house, "Bread! That this house may never know hunger. Salt! That life may always have flavor. And wine! That joy and prosperity may reign forever." She is giving without being cloying or resentful, and joyful without being in denial. She seems, from the outset, to see the greater meaning and purpose of the work they do at the building and loan. We don't know from the movie whether Mary is disdainful of money and the material world or whether she worries about "selling out"—common characteristics of the Creator/Artist. She is in many ways the true hero of the movie and appears to be the character with the most balance around money issues.

What Energy Are We Striving For?

Deborah Price adds one final archetype to her typology: the Magician. Deborah defines this as the ideal type—those who can balance the relationship between the spiritual and material world and use this balance to transform and manifest their financial reality.

I have mixed feelings about adding this final category. I tend to steer away from typologies that say, "Here's the solution. You just need to be like this." No one is going to be perfect—we all have aspects of at least most of the Money Energies within us, whether to a large extent or small. But I do agree with Deborah's point that we can learn to embrace the healthier aspects of each type. This is the spiritual practice I'm talking about. We want to be honest and engaged with our money but also spontaneous and trusting; generous and optimistic but wise and conscious; involved but fluid; living in the present moment but not in denial about the future. Balance is possible in relationship to this thing we call money, but it's not easy to attain. In fact, working on these issues is like holding a knife by the blade. Money will bring out some of the best and the worst in us, but this is of course what makes relating to it such a rich and important spiritual practice. To be completely in balance on this issue is to attain some level of enlightenment. It's a tall order for us humans, but certainly something on which to set our sights. Tools and practices can help us get there.

PRACTICE:
You and the Money Energies

It's good to know where our tendencies and patterns around money lie so we can change those that are holding us back. As I mentioned earlier, if you wish to take Deborah Price's Money Type Quiz, you can do so at her Money Coaching Institute website.

You can also look at this exercise less formally and simply write down those attributes from each Money Energy that you sense are strong in you. Be aware that if you see no attributes or very few from one particular Money Energy, this could be a clue that this represents a "shadow" for you. More on this is discussed in the next section on "Facing the Shadow."

Use this information to help yourself become aware of these attributes in your money life. If you feel one of these archetypal energies is strong in you, you might consider personifying it/him/her with a name and a visual representation. I know one woman who calls the Martyr energies in herself "the Matron." She envisions a severe woman in a shapeless black dress and a tight bun at the back of her neck. Whenever she hears the voice in her head sighing something along the lines of, "That's okay. I can do it myself," she recognizes it as the Matron's voice. If you were to personify one of your energies, what would you say to him or her? What would you ask and what would the response be? What would be revealed by such a conversation? Try doing this out loud. It might seem silly at first, but it could be insightful to see what comes up. (If this practice seems *way* too silly or embarrassing, you might ask yourself which energy this embarrassment is tapping into!)

Whether or not you choose to personify one or more of these energies, set an intention to notice what tendencies and feelings surface when you engage the monetary world: when you pay bills, make donations to charity, go over your budget, loan or borrow money, give or receive gifts, look at financial statements, charge for a service, leave a tip, make plans for retirement, talk to your parents or children about money, and so on. Which tasks leave you feeling stuck, fearful, ashamed, or angry? Which ones do you truly enjoy? Can you embrace the feelings they bring up and recognize where they are coming from? If negative feelings surface, is there something you can do differently to align these tasks in a new direction? Awareness of these attributes and patterns and an intention to change is part of the spiritual path—a journey to serenity, joy, connection, and wholeness.

Facing the Shadow

We've been exploring the ways money has played a role in and influenced our upbringing and psychological and spiritual development. This kind of direct look at the past through the lens of money is helpful. But what about the dark corners we can't or don't want to look at? What about the parts of us that exist in the realm beyond word and reason? Should reaching into these unknown places be part of the spiritual journey too? I think the answer is yes, and I found help with psychologist Bill Plotkin.

Many years ago, I was at a party where I got into a discussion with a woman about natural places we loved. She described her home in the mountains of Montana and how much she and her husband loved their cabin there. I talked about my own experiences in the natural world and how I longed for more and deeper encounters. During that conversation, she mentioned a few authors she thought I would enjoy, one of whom was Plotkin.

Soon after that discussion I bought Plotkin's book *Nature and the Human Soul: Cultivating Wholeness and Community in a Fragmented World.*[5] From the opening of the first page, I could not put it down. His nature-rooted developmental psychology spoke to me, and very soon into the book, I flipped over the jacket, thinking, "Who *is* this guy?" Bill Plotkin is a depth psychologist, but also the founder of Animus Valley Institute, which offers programs that allow participants to immerse themselves in nature and, thus, their own psyches as part of that natural world. Since then, I have read many of his books and eventually participated in the Animus retreats. They quite literally changed my life.

Plotkin offers a nature-based vision of human consciousness and relationship to soul. Like Deborah Price, Plotkin provides a description of psychic energies or archetypes in his book *Wild Mind: A Field Guide to the Human Psyche,*[6] though Plotkin's are not specifically focused on money. His premise is deep and rich, so I recommend you read it to get a full perspective of his ideas. But I want to outline his ideas briefly here as another way of looking at our relationship with money and, when necessary, working to change that relationship on our path to wholeness.

Plotkin presents a "nature-based map of the human psyche" as a model of wholeness for any natural being, which of course includes humans and their minds. He uses nature's seven directions—north, south, east, west, up, down, and center—as the basis for this three-dimensional map. If people are to embrace wholeness, they need to embrace each of these seven elements as much as possible. And even though, as I said, the ideas Plotkin presents are not related to money specifically, I have found that using this "map" to move toward wholeness in my psyche has brought with it wholeness in my relationship to money. There is the additional element of this map that assumes our innate and deep connection to nature. Admitting money into this connection instead of keeping it separate brings us one step closer to a harmonious relationship with it.

In a nutshell, Plotkin delineates the horizontal and vertical planes of the psyche. The horizontal plane includes four facets of what he calls the "Self" or our innate human potential. He uses nature's four cardinal directions to reflect these four facets: The Northern facet is the Nurturing Generative

Adult: "empathic, compassionate, courageous, competent, knowledgeable, productive, and able to provide genuine loving care and service to both ourselves and others." In the South is the Wild Indigenous One: "emotive, erotic-sexual, sensuous, instinctive, and playful." The home of the Innocent-Sage is in the East: "innocent, wise, clear-minded, light-hearted, wily, and extroverted ... fully at home with the big picture, light, enlightenment, laughter, paradox, eternity, and the mysteries of the Divine and the upperworld." Finally, the West is the facet of the Muse-Beloved: "imaginative, erotic-romantic, idealistic, visionary, adventurous, darkness savoring (shadow loving), meaning attuned, and introverted."

Because we are human, we also have wounded and immature aspects to our psyches, which run parallel to these four facets of the whole self. Plotkin calls these the "subpersonalities," which also exist on the horizontal plane within the four directions, although often they are hidden from sight. These subpersonalities may have grown from a legitimate need to keep us safe and secure, but they have outgrown their usefulness. In the North, we have the Loyal Solider, a part of ourselves stuck in the old ways of defending ourselves from perceived threats. Examples include rescuers, codependents, enablers, pleasers, and critics and flatterers—of ourselves and of others. In the South are the Wounded Children, helping us get our basic needs met with immature, emotional tactics: victims, conformists, rebels, princes, and princesses. The East is the facet of evasion and the avoidance of challenge and responsibility: Escapists and Addicts. And the West is the realm of the Shadow and our Shadow Selves, where we're kept safe through repression of either positive or negative characteristics.

The map is multidimensional, however, and therefore includes a vertical axis consisting of the Spirit and the Soul. Plotkin describes the Spirit as moving in an upward direction (toward God, Mystery, the nondual, the upperworld) and the Soul as reaching down into the depths, or into our unique and deepest individual identities. At the center, or the intersection of the horizontal and the vertical, is the Ego. This generally is our "home"—the place we inhabit on a daily basis and with which we are most comfortable. Recognizing and accepting the other facets is the work of wholeness.

There is of course much more of this map to be explored in Plotkin's book, including many practices for getting in touch with the shadowy facets of the psyche and connecting those facets to their place in the natural world. I recommend these. Here, I'll just mention that it's interesting to note the parallels between Deborah Price's Money Types and the facets of the Self and Subpersonalities that Plotkin distinguishes in his map. Whether or not you delve more deeply into either of these paradigms or both, it's imperative that we not ignore the many elements of our personality traits and our emotions, in general and when it comes to our dealings with money. Becoming aware of these elements—those on the surface and those more hidden—and accepting them for what they are is the beginning of our journey to wholeness. It's also important not to put too much of a negative spin on what we find. We are who we are for a reason and can do harm to ourselves if we pathologize the many facets that make us who we are. The point is not to suppress or eliminate, but to cultivate positive growth and wholeness.

Looking into the shadows of our psyche is by definition hard to do. This part of ourselves is in the shadows for a reason—we don't want to see it. Even though intellectually we may decide we wish to recognize our shadow side in relationship to money (or anything else), it's difficult to "think our way through" such a process. Our Ego is too cunning. In the section on Money Energies, I mentioned that it's just as important to pay attention to those attributes that are missing or in small supply in each Energy. This can be a backdoor glimpse at our shadow side.

As an example, when I assessed my own Money Energies, I thought I had no Victim attributes. My mother had those attributes—not me. I was more like my father—generally a Warrior (and every so often the Tyrant), but I also have a lot of Creator/Artist attributes. But having learned a few things about myself along the way with the help of deft guides like Price and Plotkin, I decided it might be good to investigate this supposed empty place. What I found surprised me. I realized I had, in fact, a good deal of Victim energy lurking around in the shadows. There were events in my past that had left me feeling victimized, and as I looked back into the shadows, I wasn't proud of my responses. But by looking at them in the face and not judging, I could grow. Here's one example: For years after I left the family business, and before I started my own business, I ungraciously accepted money from my father on a monthly basis. I was not grateful for the money. I felt he "owed" me for the way he had treated me during the debacle that resulted in my leaving the family business. I felt used by him and was willing to use what I perceived to be his guilt over the situation to my advantage. In this situation and others, I was using my Victim energy to justify manipulation and disloyalty, and in looking back it made me ashamed. But by looking at this shadow with honesty and accepting it, I was able to make amends, try to avoid it in the future, and use this knowledge as a step toward greater wholeness.

How do you catch your own shadow? First and foremost, you must have to *want* to catch it. And once you truly have this desire, it will start to be revealed. One way you can tell you're in the presence of the shadow is when you have a strong reaction to someone else's traits. If someone in your life *really* irritates you, especially in ways that are significantly out of proportion to how they seem to affect others, it's likely you're in the presence of your own shadow. It's an odd phenomenon that the things we most loath about others often speak volumes about ourselves. But the opposite can be true too. If you strongly admire someone, you might be in the presence of what is sometimes referred to as the Golden Shadow. The person represents aspects of yourself that, for whatever reason, you're not quite ready to accept—your own beauty or kindness or competence or humor.

Finally, I think the best way to get in touch with your shadows is to accept that you have them and to seek them out with kindness and compassion. Once you admit them, you can integrate them into your life and open them to the light. This is a critical and ongoing step in the work of becoming whole. Our shadow aspects in relationship to money are some of the darkest secrets we carry and hide, mostly from ourselves. In finding them, naming them, and working to transform them, humor and compassion are key.

To engage the shadow, it helps to bypass the rational mind by visiting planes other than language, for instance, dreams, imagination, creative movement, artwork, silence, immersion in the natural world, to name some. There are many practices that can help us move a few steps closer to the unspeakable dimensions of our hearts, the inchoate feelings circling under the surface of thought, and the parts of ourselves we tend keep in the shadows. I've included two below that may help you reach this shadow level through the use of imagination and connecting to the natural world.

PRACTICES:
Imaging Money

A Walk with Money
This practice starts with a simple walk in nature. If possible, do this in a place where you are relatively alone—in the woods, a garden, a beach, a park—but definitely out of doors in a place without others and without much distraction. This practice is similar to the one I mentioned under the Money Energies section above, but it's somewhat different. Instead of personifying one of your archetypal energies, consider personifying money itself—at least enough to take it with you on this walk. Don't spend too much time trying to come up with images or names. If

that happens, it's fine, but just let the idea settle loosely in your mind that money is meandering along with you on this walk. Don't try to overanalyze or intellectually dismember your thoughts about the process, just take money along. Wander easily, looking at the natural world around you and experiencing the sensations—the smells, the textures, the sounds. But be aware on some level that money is there with you and what sensations this additional traveler brings to the walk. If certain thoughts or emotions surface, especially strong ones, be aware of them, but don't linger too long on them. If you find yourself wishing to converse with money—either silently or out loud—please do so! But don't be too inclined to steer the conversation in a certain direction. See what you have to say to money and how money responds.

Try to spend at least twenty minutes on this walk, or longer. If it's helpful, take a few notes when you return from your journey, but this isn't necessary. The point is to become more aware in a natural and physical way of how money is affecting your walk through the world. It may also allow those aspects of your relationship with money that are usually hidden in the shadows to surface. Don't be afraid or critical of what surfaces. Just witness what arises without judgment.

Money as an Animal

This is a very simple practice and can be revealing. Ask yourself, "If money were an animal, what would it be?" Use your imagination to play with this question awhile and consider the characteristics of money and your relationship with it. What pops into your head as an animal representation of this? I've played this game, and what came to mind for me was a donkey. It's a beast of burden that helps me carry things and carry others. Another example comes from a friend who sees money as a turtle because he is slow and plodding when it comes to money. He said he also thinks of money as a "shell" of protection against perceived danger.

Play with this a bit and see what comes up.

CHAPTER 3

Looking In

Your vision will become clear only when you look inside your own heart. ... Who looks outside, dreams; who looks inside, awakes.
—CARL JUNG

W hen I decided I needed to "get up and deal with my money," I dove in. I started by doing some online research, then called my broker and asked questions. It dawned on me that I had spent most of the previous ten years reading and doing theological research. I could do the same with finances and investing. After a few conversations with my broker, he asked if I'd ever considered becoming a broker. I basically told him, trying to be kind, "I'd rather eat dirt."

He said, "Well, you know, the industry is changing. There's starting to be a bigger emphasis on financial planning. It's something you might want to think about."

Before I had completely given up on the idea of getting my PhD, I started trading stocks to make a little extra money.

One April day my eleven-year-old daughter came up to me as I scrolled the computer for trades. She asked me if it bothered me that the way I was making money had no meaningful social purpose. I responded sarcastically by asking her if having food on the table was a meaningful purpose, but I heard the message. I didn't put it this way at the time, but I knew there was something misaligned with what I was doing.

I talked to my brother Mark often during this period. He was still in the family business at that time, dealing with the frustrations I had discarded when I left. Though I was no longer connected with the family company, I had been able to maintain ties with the family and was often drawn into situations that felt toxic. Both Mark and I were also still reeling from the disastrous ergonomic-chair fiasco, both of us trying to figure out what that "failure" meant for the next steps we took.

It was a low time. My closest friend from divinity school had recently died on the eve of her thirty-fifth birthday, completely unexpectedly. I was grieving that loss, thinking about how precarious life is, and feeling anxious and unsettled about my own. So I did what a lot of us do when we're feeling low—fantasized about a vacation. That's right—let's purchase a solution! I scrolled the internet, imagining the places I could go to get away from it all. (That old flight response.) I looked at the San Juan Islands north of Seattle, Washington, because my friend who had died had spoken lovingly about those islands. I had never been there, but I booked a trip to Orcas Island.

It's not easy to get to Orcas Island. You have to *really* want it. After flying into Seattle, you must then drive two hours north to the ferry landing at Anacortes. There you wait in line for the next ferry, hoping you'll get on. The ferry ride is a ninety-minute journey through the breath-taking waterways of the Puget Sound, stopping at several forest-and-meadow-covered islands before finally arriving at Orcas.

Orcas is the largest of the San Juan Islands, a little more than fifty square miles in a saddlebag shape. It contains the islands' highest mountain peak, groves of old-growth trees, clear mountain lakes, and a spectacular view of the twelve-thousand-foot Mt. Baker on the mainland. I remember vividly stepping off the ferry for the first time and breathing in the twilight air. The late-setting sun shimmered through the Douglas firs and red madrone trees. The air felt different than anything I had ever experienced. A thought floated to the surface of my mind: "I'm home. This is what home smells like."

My immediate connection with the island was so strong and so visceral I wanted to find a way to stay connected. My Warrior mind raced forward: "What job could I do and live here?" I couldn't live there full time, but I wondered if there was a way to be there during the summers. Because of my recent dive into the world of finance, I started thinking perhaps there was a financial job I could do online. Keep in mind that this was 2001, and online capabilities were limited. There was no such thing as "wireless" back then—at least not in the mainstream. But I thought, "The technology will come along. This is just going to keep getting easier."

By my third day on the island, I was already thinking about buying property. It was a crazy idea, but I couldn't brush it away. The next morning, I walked down to the bay alone and strolled along the pebbled shore, looking out at the silver mist still clinging to the trees. I was thinking about the possibility of buying property and feeling torn between the insanity of the idea and the intense feeling that it was the right thing to do. "Show me where I belong," I asked God, the universe, myself. The tide was out, so I walked across the wet strip of land to a tiny island with a few fir trees on it. I sat down on a stone and looked out across the calm water. Suddenly, I heard a *whoosh, whoosh, whoosh* above me, and an eagle flew up and perched in one of the trees, looking down at me. I stared at the huge creature in astonishment. Then I heard another *whoosh, whoosh, whoosh*, and a second eagle appeared, landing right next to the first one. They both peered down at me with only slight interest, and I felt something shift in me. For the first time in my life, I felt a conscious connection with these magnificent creatures and all the creatures in our world. I looked at the eagles and thought, "These are real beings, and they're looking at me. But they're also looking through me because I'm not that special. I'm one of many, but I do have a place here." It was a sense of being properly located on the earth—neither more nor less than anyone else, but deeply grounded. That morning, I had a profound recognition that the natural world—especially this place—was a conduit for my connection to the divine.

Later that day, we looked at property and made an offer on a moss-and-tree-covered piece of land high up the side of a mountain. My partner thought I was out of my mind and was not totally wrong. I had little money left and no clear career path. But I was convinced that whatever I did, Orcas Island had to be part of it. We closed on the property that fall.

Of course, then I really needed a job. I looked into the idea of becoming a broker, but decided instead to become a financial planner. I studied, took the exams, and went on board with a national firm, ready to see clients in August 2002. I chose financial planning because it seemed the most holistic approach to money—a mixture of nuts-and-bolts planning, investment advice, behavior modification, counseling, and pastoral care.

While I was doing the traditional financial planning studies, I also read George Kinder's book *The Seven Stages of Money Maturity.*[1] Kinder is the originator of what has come to be called the "Life Planning Movement," which focuses on the human or heart side of money. This book profoundly influenced my view of the financial industry and got me thinking. I knew I was wounded and confused when it came to money, and it occurred to me that others probably were, too. It seemed that financial planning could be a way to help others seek a deeper level of integration around these issues, and it aligned with my diverse background, including my religious studies.

Once we have taken an honest look at our past, our wounds, and our tendencies around money, it becomes easier to look at our relationships with money in the present moment. In hindsight, I see that I was doing this very thing in my own life as I "got up and dealt with my money." It didn't occur to me at the time to think of it as spiritual practice, but I now see that it was—or, at least it was evolving into a spiritual practice. Most people start asking these bigger questions as they move along their life paths: "How much time do I have to spend on this journey, and what's it for anyway?

Am I accomplishing anything important or worthy? How do I tap into something deeper than the mundane tasks of my day?" This is the bedrock of the spiritual path, and money is there.

Any practice that cultivates our connection with the deeper soul within us, or as some call it, the divine, is a spiritual practice. Any practice that moves us away from our usual dualistic thinking that claims people, nature, God, "the outside world" are separate from us is spiritual practice. Any practice that makes us more comfortable with mystery and questions and taps into a wellspring of love and compassion is spiritual practice. There are many such practices. For some, they are connected to a religious tradition, such as prayer, meditation, fasting, reading religious texts, chanting, yoga, pilgrimages, retreats, and many others; this is not an exhaustive list. It may also include artwork, dance, martial arts, singing, journaling, study and contemplation on a particular subject, poetry, and walking in nature, to name a few. Even mundane tasks such as washing dishes, folding laundry, or weeding a garden can be a spiritual practice if it's done with intention and draws us into a deeper, more meaningful place of oneness with time, space, and others. However, I've yet to find a list of spiritual practices that includes going over the budget with a spouse or talking with a financial planner about retirement plans. As I've made my own journey with money, I've grown in the realization that this must change.

If we believe in the ultimate interconnectedness of all reality, and I do, money cannot be divorced from this reality and, therefore, our practice. The goal is to have our money lives align with our spiritual lives—our heart center. The first step, then, must be an exploration of that heart center—what it looks like, what feeds it, and the direction it is pointing.

Money and Time

As tempting as it would be to start with something light and easy here, I think it's best to go ahead and jump into the thorniest issue first: money and time, or rather, our lack of it. Despite all our attempts to avoid it, we all live with the certain knowledge of our own deaths. As I described in chapter 1, arguably the ultimate power money has over us as individuals and our money system is its finely honed ability to deny mortality. This is not all show either. Money does help put off death—sometimes. Money can buy medicine, good food, health care, and so on. There's a lot of power in that. The problem is when we use money to keep us from facing the fact that ultimately no amount of money will keep us from dying. We can either live in total denial and fear of that fact or live in relationship with it.

Looking death square in the face is one of the oldest spiritual practices. Some of the monastic mothers and fathers would sit in caves staring at skulls, contemplating the reality of death. I'm not suggesting we need to take up that practice exactly, but there may be something in such a contemplation that is comforting—to know we are not alone on our journey but part of a larger reality. It also can help us focus on our heart center and what truly matters for the time we have left.

Time is the other side of the coin of death. If time were not limited, we would necessarily look at our lives very differently.

Think about it: If you were going to live forever, all you would need to worry about was finding a way to provide for yourself and your loved ones *today*. There would be no such thing as tomorrow or yesterday—there would only be the ever present *now*. You would not need to purchase things just because you might need them later. You would not need to save money because you would not get old and wouldn't need money put aside for the future when you couldn't work. You would not need to worry about leaving a "legacy" of money to those left behind, because you would always be around to make more of it or provide for yourself and others. In fact, it's hard to imagine whether there would be *any* need for money if we didn't have to worry about the future—about time. After all, one of our culture's motto's is "Time *is* money."

The prospect of not being able to work anymore in the future is what drives people to set aside money for retirement. Well, we used to call it *retirement*, but that word is falling out of use. Because people are living so much longer than they used to, they're either working longer or transitioning into new careers or jobs—paid or unpaid. But the point is that people feel the need to set aside money to live on (a nest egg) once they can't or choose not to work for money. When people engage a financial planner these days, most of the time they want to make sure they have enough money to quit working for money. And most are doing it because they would like *some* time to stop working for money before they die. Really, that's the bottom line. If they knew precisely when they were going to die, a financial planner could tell them exactly how much they would need to save, assuming they could maintain a certain spending pattern.

If we knew for a fact when we were going to die, would it affect how we use the time we have left? Maybe—maybe not. It might, if it took away some of the fear factor. When we talk about spending money or giving to others out of generosity, we sometimes hold back. Why? Fear of the future. "What if I give away so much that I'm vulnerable and there's nobody there to take care of me?" I'm not trying to imply that people shouldn't be saving for the future or proactive about their future. This is a legitimate concern. But living a life based on fear is not the answer. We "spend" money, and we "spend" time, but sometimes it feels like each is spending us. The seductive message of our money system is that if we just get (purchase or accumulate, or both) a bit more, the fear will go away. The more you have, the less likely you are to suffer, to die. The problem is we don't know how much is enough, and we feel in our deepest heart of hearts this uncertainty of our existence. Many things can befall us and the ones we love. We think that if we have money, we will have more choices, maybe even a little power over outcomes. But how true is that? And is it worth it? To refer again to Joe Dominguez's definition of money as "something we choose to trade our life energy for," are we really "saving" our lives by "saving" money? While it is possible to make more money, you cannot, under any circumstances, make more time. Think about the weight of our society's motto "Time is money." Is this an adage you live by? Is that the only way? Consider the motto of the tiny country of Bhutan. According to Karma Tshiteem, secretary of the Bhutan Gross National Happiness Commission, their motto is "Time is life."[2] Does that ring true?

This dilemma is a complex one with no correct or easy answer. But it helps no one to pretend the dilemma does not exist. We must look at it square in the face and with courage.

PRACTICE:
An Experiment with Time

As I mentioned earlier in this chapter, George Kinder's book *The Seven Stages of Money Maturity* had a profound influence on my exploration of money and its relationship to the heart. In that book Kinder advocates asking ourselves some key questions in order to discern what truly matters to us. Once that is articulated, we can then work to deploy our financial resources in that direction. The practice below was taken from Kinder's ideas on this topic, which I've tweaked slightly based on my own experiences working with individuals and groups over the years.

So here we go:

Let's do a thought experiment. This doesn't have to be done in a cave holding a skull (though it wouldn't hurt), but it's helpful if you allow yourself some quiet, uninterrupted time to think about the scenarios below.

Once you have had time to think about them, write down whatever emerges. Writing is important in this instance because the words themselves may help "incarnate," or make real, a vision for your life.

- Let's say today you find out you have five to ten years to live. You won't be debilitated; you will simply die suddenly within that time frame. Think about it for a while. What would you change about your life? What would stay the same? What choices would you make? In what new direction would you turn? What are the money implications of your decisions?
- After mulling that over for a while, consider that instead you only have one year to live. Does that change any of the answers to your questions? What would your ideal day look like in such a scenario?
- Finally, consider the idea that you will die before sundown today. Now what does your day look like? What are you regretting that you didn't do? Who did you not become?

How do you ultimately want to "spend" whatever time you have left? How do you want to impact the world? And conversely, what doesn't really matter? We all know that moment when we find out someone we love is hurt or sick. All the extraneous stuff goes out the window, and we become sharp as a tack. Things that seemed important ten minutes earlier suddenly have little or no meaning. That's the power of this kind of clarity and focus. On the other hand, some who experiment with this may find they are doing exactly what they want to be doing and would change nothing. This is important knowledge to have as well.

This practice is just a thought experiment. I don't want to present it as more profound than that. People change over time, and their goals and insights change—this is the nature of living. But try it and see if it helps you assess whether the outer structures of your life—including your financial structures—are aligned with your inner life and heart center. Write down any insights that come to you. They may be road signs worth paying attention to and may be a good starting point to some of the practices later in this chapter.

Your Courageous Vision

Here's the good news: You're not dead yet! You still have *time*, and there are steps you can take to change direction or go deeper on your path, if you so choose. If that last practice stirred something in you or evoked the spark of a vision—small or large—trust it. Look at the words you wrote down. Is there an inkling of a way to go deeper on your journey coming to light, or a different path that more closely aligns with your heart center? Allow yourself to boldly imagine this vision. A lot of people have trouble with this. They have a difficult time visualizing a new direction, much less taking steps to bring it to fruition, for fear of being disappointed or laughed at by others or internally. This is the moment for courage—to move beyond this fear with trust in your vision and the recognition of its power and importance. This beacon is what I call your "courageous vision." The beginnings of it might be quite small—a realization that you want to add a morning walk or a five-minute meditation to your routine or change your eating habits. Or it may seem like the seed of something grander, like changing your career or how you spend your money. Whatever it is, trust it. Even if you feel only the initial stirrings of this vision, follow it. Remember what Martin Luther King Jr. said: "Faith is taking the first step even when you don't see the whole staircase."[3]

The practices listed below are meant to help you tap into that vision and tease it out. I use the term *courageous vision*, though in some cases this will not be a new vision or path but a deepening of the path you are already on. All of us are growing at every moment. These practices are designed to help you pay attention to that growth in your life with the help of your gifts and heart's desires, explore the direction in which you are being called by that growth, and discern how you want to respond.

PRACTICE:
Identifying Your Gifts and Talents

All of us are born with certain gifts and talents, some of which are cultivated and encouraged, and some of which are not. We may also hone certain traits during our lives and turn them into what we commonly refer to as a "talent." Some of these may be obvious—singing, cooking, writing, research, public speaking, and so on. But other talents may not be as obvious, or we may dismiss them as unimportant. For instance, can you make people laugh? Are you organized? Are you good with plants or animals? Are you a sympathetic listener? Can you finish a crossword puzzle in record time? Recognizing and embracing your true gifts and talents is an important step in deepening your relationship with yourself and aligning those talents with your courageous vision.

For people who have been brought up to believe that acknowledging your own talents is wrong or boastful (there are several religious traditions that foster this idea), this can be a difficult task. But it's important not only to think about these things but also to reinforce them in some way by writing them down, creating a collage of them, drawing a picture of them, or creating some other tangible representation. This may seem unnecessary—even silly, but this simple act can have an amazing ability to encourage those talents and help them foster your journey.

Like with the other practices, you'll want to carve out some space and time for this exercise. Think about your strengths—what you're good at and what you enjoy. If you're not sure what you have a "knack" for, it might help to think about times when others have told you that you're good at something or times you've succeeded at something that made you joyful. Make a list of these talents and gifts and keep it in a place where you can refer to it from time to time. If you prefer, draw a picture that represents these gifts or create some other piece of artwork. Some people enjoy creating a collage. It's easy and strangely satisfying to do this. Gather four or five old magazines around you that you don't mind cutting up, along with some scissors, a glue stick, and a piece of paper or cardboard. Flip through the magazines with no particular agenda other than the loose idea that you want to celebrate your gifts and talents. Cut out anything that pops out as significant without giving it much thought, if any. It might be words or phrases or pictures. If it grabs you, cut it or tear it out. No need to be neat and tidy. When you have a nice pile, look them over and take out the ones you want to use. Or just start gluing them onto your paper or cardboard. You might glue them on randomly or create some sort of picture or poem with them, but don't give it too much thought. If it makes you happy, you can trim the cutouts for clean lines, but only if you find joy in that. When you've finished your project, look at it to see what themes appear. Remember that this is not a piece of artwork for you or others to judge; it is a message. What is it telling you? Are you surprised by anything? Keep it in a place where you can revisit it from time to time. It can be a reminder to celebrate your best traits, or you may see a totally new message you didn't notice before.

Your gifts and talents are important, but why? Because they can and should serve what you value. The dictionary defines "values" as "a person's principles or standards of behavior; one's judgment of what is important in life." Most of us have a general idea of what we value but rarely give it focused attention. Being honest and clear with ourselves by acknowledging what and who we value is part of the spiritual path. This task was addressed to some extent in chapter 2, when we talked about our Money Energies. With those Money Energies in mind, we can directly define our values and their place in our heart center. Once we are clear on this, we can more easily serve them and our courageous vision through our gifts and talents. The next practice is designed to look directly at values.

PRACTICE:
Identifying Who and What You Value

A common practice for identifying your values is to think about defining moments in your life when you felt truly happy, fulfilled, proud, centered, or some combination of these. Think about the details of one or more of those moments: What were you doing? Who were you with? What contributed to those deeply positive feelings? Are there other details that seem related? Once you've given this some thought, write down the values that came up—the "whos" as well as the "whats." If you prefer to look at a list of values from which to choose, there are plenty available on the internet, but it's also good to name your own.

When I think of a defining moment in my own life, I think of my first trip to Orcas Island with my family, and in particular, that day when the two eagles visited me. The values this event brings into focus for me are

- connection to the natural world;
- beauty;
- holiness;
- solitude;
- compassion for and connection to others; and
- love.

Other defining moments have brought up different (though related) values for me:

- service, or helping others
- joy
- education
- openness
- hard work

I suggest coming up with a list of at least ten values. It can also be instructive to narrow this down (if possible) to the top three or four, just to see what comes into focus. Being clear with yourself about what's most important to you can help you align them with the choices you make.

As part of this practice, I also recommend identifying the people you value. You'll probably automatically put your family and friends on your list, but I suggest you pause first and give this real thought. Who specifically do you value, and why? Be honest with yourself. (You don't have to show this list to anyone.) In addition to the people you know, are there people you don't know personally whom you value? Why do you value them? Is there anyone you specifically do *not* value? Why not? Does this list help you streamline your list of values?

With these practices, you have been bringing to your awareness the various elements of your courageous vision: a general or perhaps specific direction in which your heart is guiding you, the gifts and talents you have to aid you in your journey, and the values you will be serving along the way. This is the bedrock of your spiritual path. Don't worry if your vision seems vague or evolving. The truth is it will always be evolving. These practices are a way of being an active and aligned part of that evolution. You start by putting your gaze upon it and being honest with yourself about what you see. Then you follow the path as best you can, creating as you go. A central tenant of the Christian religion is "incarnation"— God interpenetrating humanity and the world through "the word made flesh," or "spirit incarnate." Similarly, we can be proactive in the creation of our own path and vision. As with the last two practices, creating a physical representation of this vision—whether it is through words or artwork or some other representation—can help create it.

PRACTICE:

Incarnating Your Vision

There are two possible practices in this section. As with all the other practices, allow yourself time, space, creativity, and an open mind.

This practice is similar to the one for identifying your gifts and talents. You'll start by asking yourself some questions: How would I describe my spiritual path today? Do I even think I'm on such a path? Am I following that path the way I want to? Do I have a courageous vision for my future? If so, what does that vision look like? Who does it involve? How does it impact others? Are changes needed? If so, what? Does my courageous vision look or feel like something in particular? How do I feel when I think about this vision? You may think of other questions as you go.

Follow up this thought exercise by writing down your answers so you can refer back to them. If a vision is coming to the surface, write down whatever appears without worrying if all the pieces fit together or whether it's "right." Perhaps these words could be turned into a poem or a piece of prose. Artwork is another great way to articulate this vision—a collage or a drawing—something you can look back at from time to time. Don't worry if you don't consider yourself "artsy"; this is about the process and the message that emerges, not creating a framed work of art. Make time to be creative with this practice—just make it real somehow, knowing you're free to update it or change it as your vision evolves. There is no right or wrong here. Rest assured, your path will change and flow over time. The practice is for helping the nuggets of your vision work their way to the surface.

I had a friend who looked for a new job for a year. She had worked for twenty-five years in the nonprofit sector, so she assumed her new job would be in that arena—and that's where she looked, but nothing panned out. Just for fun, she created a new-job collage. With no more direction than that, she flipped through several magazines and cut out pictures and words that jumped out at her. Then she glued them together into a collage. In stepping back and looking at it, these elements emerged: new challenges, connecting with people she could relate to, putting her writing and organizational skills to good use, and serving the wider community. Three phrases particularly jumped out to her: "Leave ordinary behind," "Can you imagine it?" and "Make yourself at home." This collage did not tell her what job to look for or even what might be out there, but it did open the space in her mind for something beyond her current limited scope. Soon after, she took a very different position than the ones she had been considering, and it met the criteria her collage had pointed to as important. Interestingly, though she had never considered doing so before, in this position she worked from home and loved it. Her collage knew before she did.

The other practice that some may find helpful in this visioning process is a guided meditation. It's a way of opening some different doors in the mind and perhaps finding an unexpected passage to your interior. Some find this type of exercise helpful, others not so much, but it's worth experimenting with. Though it's not necessary, you might want to have someone else read the words out loud to you as you meditate, or record yourself reading the words and play it as you meditate.

> Find a comfortable seated position—on the floor, on a cushion, in a chair—or you can do this lying down. To the extent that you can, try to keep your spine straight but not stiff, or find a position that will support your straight posture. Close your eyes and take several easy breaths, noticing that without any effort your breath gradually becomes deeper and longer.
>
> As your mind settles, imagine you are walking slowly along an easy path through a sun-dappled forest. The trees are tall and covered in green leaves, but the canopy is not so thick that you can't see the blue sky above from time to time. Sunlight streams through the branches onto the forest floor, which is thick with soft, green moss and delicate ferns. The air is clean with the slightest kiss of a breeze. Your walk is slow and easy. Soon you see a figure coming toward you on the path. It's an older man

walking with a carved wooden cane, but he moves with lightness and ease. His face is friendly as he notices you and looks into your eyes. As you draw closer to him, you see he is carrying a large, hardback book in his other hand. When he is quite close to you he greets you by name and holds the book out to you.

"I've been waiting to give this to you," he says. "Take a look now but hold onto it so you can read it in depth later." You take the book from him, thanking him. He passes you and moves on down the path with no other words. You look down at the book but there is nothing on the cover. You open to the first page. What do you see? [PAUSE] Are there words? Pictures? Both? [PAUSE] Flip through the pages. What catches your eye on first glance? [PAUSE]

You close the book and continue down the path. Soon you hear the sound of water and notice a small brook meandering through the forest near your path. The water tumbles easily over the stones in its way. As you walk along the path the brook grows a little larger and the sound of water intensifies. You soon reach an opening in the trees where there is a pool of clear water beneath a small waterfall. Surrounding the pool are white flowers and soft grass. There is a woman standing at the edge of the pool. She turns and looks at you, and she too looks directly into your eyes with kindness. "I'm glad you're here," she says. "There is something I've been wanting to tell you—something you've been needing to hear. Come over and let me tell you." You walk over to the woman and stand next to her. She cups her hand around your ear and whispers her message. [PAUSE] What did she whisper to you? Does it have any meaning to you? How does it make you feel? [PAUSE]

The woman smiles at you and turns to leave. "Pay attention," she says and walks away. You stare after her, thinking about the message she has given you and what it might mean. You're not sure. You decide to lie down on the soft grass next to the pool to think about it. The sun is warm here and the sound of the water is soothing. You soon find yourself getting drowsy, so you close your eyes. It doesn't take long before you fall asleep and begin dreaming. [PAUSE] Who are the characters in your dream? What is the scenery? Do any feelings emerge or interesting story lines? [LONG PAUSE]

It's time to awaken from your dream now. Open your eyes and come back to your room. Notice your breathing and how you feel. Wiggle your fingers and toes. Relish the little journey you've just taken.

Did this guided meditation bring up any interesting messages, road signs, symbols, or characters related to your courageous vision? Even if it seems like only a frivolous exercise, you might want to mull it over for a while and see if any puzzle pieces begin to click together. Again, I suggest you write it down. If you look at it later, a different message might emerge. If nothing came up for you, this might be a message in itself.

Once you have a seed of your courageous vision in your line of sight, you will be amazed at how it can grow, if you pay attention. This is why it helps to "incarnate" your vision in some way—with artwork or words or something else tangible. Such incarnation can help you recognize signs and symbols that speak to your vision. Try to remember any dreams you have while you're sleeping that seem to relate, and write them down. Listen to what they're telling you. Pay attention to uncanny happenings that may be leading you in a certain direction. This is the heartbeat of the soul—the "feeling of home," and you're tapping into it. Spiritual teacher Eckhart

Tolle refers to this idea in his book *A New Earth: Awakening to Your Life's Purpose*:

> When you yield internally, when you surrender, a new dimension of consciousness opens up. If action is possible or necessary, your action will be in alignment with the whole and supported by creative intelligence, the unconditioned consciousness which in a state of inner openness you become one with. Circumstances and people then become helpful, cooperative. Coincidences happen. If no action is possible, you rest in the peace and inner stillness that come with surrender. You rest in God.[4]

Personally, I'm a bit leery of the idea that we all have a particular "life's purpose." But I do believe the direction of our lives and the choices we make can be more or less aligned with spirit, love, compassion, God. If this is something you yearn for, you must pay attention to this alignment. This is what I think Tolle is describing here. This is the practice of aligning and deepening our spiritual path.

Aligning Your Money with Your Vision

Beginning to understand your feelings and patterns around money can enhance your relationship with your financial life. Understanding your gifts, and the values and heart-centered goals toward which you want to enlist those gifts, helps you articulate your courageous vision. Now, how do you weave those together?

I know a couple—I'll call them Sarah and John—who, I believe, exemplify a healthy fusion of money and the spiritual path. This is just one example, of course, and not a perfect one (there is no perfection, just practice), but it may be helpful as an illustration. Both Sarah and John grew up in families of modest income. Though neither family was highly privileged financially, they were privileged in other areas, namely education and service. These values were cherished in both of their nuclear families and were passed onto their children. Sarah and John both went to college and graduate school, with the help of student loans. When they got out of school, they were both in debt, though not at the level that is all too common in this day and age. They married soon after graduating. Like a lot of recently married couples, they struggled some with how to combine the various elements of their lives, including their finances. They told me that when they first got married, they tried to segment their finances in three ways: John's, Sarah's, and both together. Soon they realized the arrangement was too cumbersome. They combined accounts, but made it a habit to talk openly about how their money would be earned and spent. They both took what I'd call good, entry-level jobs in their professions and bought a small house, adding a mortgage to their financial picture. They didn't always agree about financial decisions, but they did try to communicate their preferences with each other and work for compromise.

During this time, Sarah and John weren't just earning and spending money; they had a social life and a growing spiritual life. They started attending a church that promoted the values that were important to them. They told me years later that it was, in fact, their involvement in the church that got them thinking about changing their careers to more service-oriented work. They began to investigate this possibility. Eventually they made the decision to quit their middle-income jobs and sell their house to move to a rural area in Central Appalachia. John took a job with a nonprofit that paid about half the salary he had been making, and Sarah began doing freelance work. They didn't make this decision lightly, by any means. Living in a house was still important to them, as was having food on the table and health care and certain things they wanted and needed to purchase. They definitely considered money in the equation, but they also considered the direction their hearts were leading them. They made this move and lived and worked in that area for several years, and had their children there. They will tell you that they struggled during this time in their lives: financially, emotionally, and physically. But they will also tell you it was worth it. They found joy and companionship and fulfillment in their lives there. They believed in what they were doing and made it work.

After several years, they made the decision to change again. Among other things, John had been diagnosed with a chronic illness, and they felt it was important that he have access to better medical care. John found another job in a less rural area, still at a nonprofit but somewhat higher paying, so they moved again. Sarah worked part-time, also at a nonprofit. They were doing work that was important to them, but weighing their enjoyment in their work with their financial needs. They also spent time, and money of course, on things they enjoyed, such as travel, when it was feasible. When the children got close to college age, Sarah took a full-time job at a for-profit business. Years before, they had made the decision that they wanted to pay for their children's college education without the children incurring debt, if that was at all possible. They told their children that this was their goal, and that any education beyond college would be the child's responsibility. By Sarah taking the new job and the kids holding part-time jobs during college, they were able to meet that goal. Articulating it in advance was key to making it work.

John and Sarah are the first to admit that their story is partly about privilege and good fortune. Though they did not grow up in wealthy families, both had the privilege of education and security. They were also willing to work for what they believed in. This—along with a bit of "being in the right place at the right time"—allowed them to get jobs when they needed them. But not all of it was luck. They thought about their values as well as their money and made decisions weighing all of it and the interconnection with their spiritual path. They took some risks. They saved for retirement but didn't focus all their attention on that. When they didn't have much money, they figured out ways to live without it, though this wasn't easy. When they did have it, they saved some for retirement and education, spent some on things they wanted and experiences with other people, and gave some away. They are still doing this today—doing their best not to deny or live in constant fear of the need for money, but at the same time not letting money run the show.

Sarah and John's story is much more complicated than what's presented here. And like I said, this is just an example of one couple's journey of avoiding extreme resource guarding or denial and balancing money needs with other needs. There are as many ways to practice this balance as there are people, and it will look different for everyone. It is possible to keep money's enormous influence in our society from consuming everything we do. If we understand ourselves and our courageous vision, we can begin to align our money activities with them. The four key money activities are earning, giving, spending, and storing. The practices below are designed to explore these activities and help create that alignment.

Earning

For most of us, our money comes by "earning" it. We perform a job, for which we are given money. Of course, money can also come through inheritance and other means, but this is the most common way of getting money in our culture. Figuring out how to earn money is not simple. Many factors play into the decision. For some, there is very little choice. We do what we have to do. But no matter how little choice we believe we have in how we earn an income, it's critical that we recognize how much, if at all, that earning is aligned with our courageous vision. Very few people, if any, are able to earn a living that is perfectly aligned with their vision. Still, it's key to at least be honest with ourselves about this and to strive for as close an alignment as we can.

It's also important not to do things that truly violate the core of our courageous vision. If environmental issues are really important to you, you might want to avoid working for a nuclear power company, for instance. This may seem obvious, and for many people, it's hard to make these decisions because of their circumstances. But it also may be because they have not yet clarified their courageous vision. That is why we focused on that first. Once this becomes clear, we ask ourselves: "Does my work serve my courageous vision?" and "Is my work valued by the members of my tribe? Do the people I earn my money from value me?" If the answer to these questions is no, you may want to work toward a change in how you earn your money. Your goal is serving your courageous vision and working for "your people." You may never fulfill this goal to the level you'd like, but working toward it is part of the spiritual practice.

The good news is that spirit doesn't care that much one way or another about bricks and mortar. It's not just about what you do for a living, but how you live. There are many ways to serve your vision and your people. You will know your vision is becoming more aligned when the people you earn money from value you and show that they value you through your earning. I'm not saying they will make you rich; but one way they will show your value is by not letting you starve. Increased alignment will also manifest itself in more contentment and ease while working and a sense of working for the "greater good."

PRACTICE:
Dream Big

Most of us end up in the jobs we have for a variety of reasons—it's what we trained to do, a family member told us to go into this line of work, it morphed from the first job we got after school, it was the easiest or the only job we could find, and so on. Many of us like some aspects of our jobs and dislike others. This is the nature of work, as well as life in general. But just for the fun of it, let's try an experiment where we imagine something else. Taking money out of the equation just for a moment, what would you do during the day? If you're stressed out and overworked at the moment, you might be tempted to answer "sleep" or "sit on the beach." But let's say you're rested up and back from vacation, ready to jump into what's next. What would you do? How would you structure your day? Would you choose to learn something new? If so, what? Who would you be with? What would you accomplish or create, if anything? How does it fit with your gifts, talents, and values? How would you feel during the day, and when you're finished? Right now, don't constrain yourself by anything. Dream big! This is just for the pure joy of it.

That's all there is to this practice: dreaming big. I do recommend "incarnating" this dream (as I've said before), no matter how outlandish it seems. Write it down or create an artistic representation of it. Come back to it from time to time and look at it. Maybe you will begin to see aspects of this dream that could be incorporated into paid work. Be open to that possibility, but don't start with that. There will likely be too many voices at the outset telling you what is and is not possible. Those voices are not invited to this practice. They'll have plenty of time to speak later. This practice is for the voice that rarely gets heard. Let it speak.

Spending

Why do we earn money? To spend it. Sure, we save some too—but that's mostly so we can spend it later, or give to someone so they can spend it. We all spend our money differently. This is one of the reasons people are afraid to talk about money in our culture: There is a lot of judgment about how we perceive others spending their money. As I write this section, US Representative Jason Chaffetz (R-Utah) is in the news for criticizing certain people for purchasing iPhones instead of spending money on their health care.[5] Many people agree with this judgment, though many also disagree with it. The point is, most of us judge others on how we see them spending their money. Looking at our own judgments about others' spending and teaching ourselves to move out of that place of judgment is part of the spiritual path.

We also need to look at our own spending. Spending can be a powerful tool and can be a direct way to exercise the muscle of your courageous vision. Do your purchases support your vision? Do you make conscious decisions when you spend? Are you truly satisfied by your purchases? Do they support and protect the planet, or the opposite? Do they serve the greater community? Do you feel grateful to those from whom you make purchases and for the goods and services you buy? And what do you do with something you no longer want? Do you throw it in the landfill, sell it on eBay, give it away? Sometimes it seems easier just to accumulate things than to exert the energy it would take to align these practices with your vision, but at what cost?

PRACTICE:
Bill Paying as Spiritual Teaching

Start this practice with an open heart and compassion for yourself, not judgment. Open your checkbook register or latest bank statement and your latest credit card statements, if you have any, or look at it online. Look at the purchases you made in the last month. What purchases brought you joy and a sense of gratitude? Which purchases made you feel guilty or resentful? Were any of them impulse buys you later regretted? What resources were used in the making of these purchases? Do you even know? Think about the interactions you had with the person from whom you bought those goods—if there was a person involved. Are you grateful to them for what they provided or do you feel cheated and bitter? Do you feel like your purchases reflect your courageous vision? If not, are there changes you could make to align your purchases with your vision? Remember to start with small steps. This practice also works if you have a budget for your household. Ask yourself these same questions as you go over the budget. If you do these tasks with a partner, discuss them with each other. If you have a regular practice of paying bills, looking at your financial statements, or going over your budget, consider beginning with a short meditation with the intention of moving into a space of gratitude.

Giving

For many, giving is an afterthought. The more focus we put on our courageous vision, though, the more giving becomes a deliberate piece of that vision. I had an elderly friend who lived alone on a modest fixed income. She was very clear on her courageous vision and wanted what little extra money she had to support that vision. She had the practice of each month giving away whatever small amount of money she had left over after paying her bills. She had an array of causes she supported and spread the money around to all of them. Each month there was a different amount to give away, but this was the discipline of her spiritual practice. It also brought her joy.

In spite of a general idea in our society that "money will buy you happiness," studies don't support this premise. At least, spending money on yourself doesn't seem to have much to do with your own happiness. Instead, spending money on others does. A series of experiments performed in North America in 2008 found that people who gave money away reported a higher level of happiness than those who spent it on themselves. The dollar amount didn't matter—it was the act of giving that brought up these positive feelings.[6]

Pay a lot of attention to this part of your money life. When you give, is it out of obligation or because it serves your courageous vision? What courageous visions of other people or organizations do you support? Do these visions align with your own? Does it serve the wider community? Do you give freely or with trepidation? Does it make you feel joyful or afraid? Are there strings attached to your giving? There is no point in giving out of a sense of guilt or because you think you should. Giving should also not be confused with controlling. Be wary of giving money in order to force someone or an organization to do something specific. I'm not saying we shouldn't be well informed about where our money is going and what it's supporting. On the contrary, this is key to the giving process. But giving as part of your courageous vision is more about gratitude and the act of sharing than manipulating an outcome.

Finally, it's important to remember that giving isn't just about writing a check or donating through PayPal. Giving also means donating time and energy. This kind of giving is also part of the spiritual path.

PRACTICE:
Gratitude Journal

Giving grows naturally from gratitude, whether it's giving money, time, or anything else. But gratitude does not come naturally for many of us. It's a frame of mind that's cultivated through practice. There are many ways to cultivate gratitude. Some people spend a few moments each morning or each evening meditating on the people, experiences, and things in their life for which they are grateful. This can be a wonderful way to start or end the day. Another way is to keep a gratitude journal. Using either a calendar with some space to write or a blank journal, make a practice of writing down at least three things for which you're grateful each day. If you do this in the morning and can't think of three things you're grateful for, that might be the impetus to make something happen that will bring you gratitude.

As you make gratitude part of your daily practice, you should find that giving flows more naturally for you and feeds your courageous vision. As part of this practice, look back at the picture or description of your courageous vision you created earlier. How can you give part of yourself away to serve that vision? Try it—a little bit at a time—and see how you feel. If you feel energized, light, joyful, centered, that's a sign that your giving practice is serving your courageous vision.

Storing

How you store your money also needs to align with your courageous vision. It matters because the act of storing money means someone else is holding it and making money by holding it, so you must think about who you're supporting through this process. What about your bank? Are you supporting the "dark lords of banking" or a credit union? And what about your investments? If you're investing money in a company or a pool of companies (mutual funds), what's under the hood there? Do you know what you're supporting or do you never look at your portfolio? If you own shares in a company, do you practice shareholder voting to influence the operations of the company? Do you run your investments through a socially conscious screening (corporate practices that promote environmental stewardship, consumer protection, human rights, and diversity)? More and more people are using such screenings, which means it's getting easier to find these kinds of investments.

Actually what we're finding is that companies that pay attention to how they affect the environment, are supportive of the communities in which they operate, and govern their businesses with openness and visibility, can tend to do better over time from an investment profitability standpoint. It didn't used to be that way, but it's changing. For one thing, these companies tend to get sued less often, so there's less money going out the door to lawyers, claimants, and so on.

When you're looking at your finances, remember that money begets money. Does your money beget resources that support your courageous vision?

PRACTICE:
Researching Where Your Money Is Stored

Most people don't give a lot of thought to where they store their money, or they believe they have little or no choice in the matter, so this practice is practical. It simply involves carving out some time (start with an hour, but you'll likely need more) to research your options. There are many things to think about: your banking institution, where your money is invested, what credit card companies you use, etc. Investigate online how these institutions themselves use their (your) money. If you can't find it online, call them and ask—or write a letter to the company. If you use a financial advisor or some other financial service, ask your advisor these questions. Gather your data. Don't get overwhelmed with this process. Do as little or as much as you're able at a time. Be kind to yourself in this process, but challenge yourself to do it.

If you find you'd like to make a change in how your money is stored, talk to others you know about what institutions they use and why. Of course you will have to weigh the consequences of change. Change will necessarily require some work and energy. Maybe there will be some fee changes. Maybe you'll have to drive a little farther to bank, or give up a service or two. Once you have the data, you can weigh these consequences with the strength of your desire to change. Or maybe you can't change now, but want to make this a goal for the future. Living without this information is one practice. Learning the truth and considering a change to align with your courageous vision is another.

You'll be engaged with the four key money activities your entire life, so aligning it with your courageous vision will be a lifelong practice. Along the way, you may want to make some changes. These changes may be small or large, numerous or just a few, but the point is to pay attention to them. You will know they are aligned when they feed your sense of peace and wholeness, rather than negativity and anxiety, and you feel like you are "coming home." As one of my friends says, "You'll know you are there when you no longer feel as if you're pushing the river."

Let me give you one example of a change a couple made to their family budgeting process. After doing some work around their money life together, they acknowledged they both felt stressed every time they went through the monthly budget together. They would end up getting into a fight each time. Once they recognized this pattern, they talked about why it happened, realizing it brought up basic fears for their future. Their answer (wisely) was not to give up doing a monthly budget, but instead to change the way they approached it. First, they developed a "serenity budget." If something happened (such as one of them lost their job), this bare-bones budget showed them that they could indeed survive. Interestingly, this budget helped them see how little they really needed for their essentials. Second, they wrote certain "serenity reminders" into this budget, so they would remember how and why they developed it. Here are a couple of examples: "This emergency budget reminds us that even in a worst case job scenario we can continue to live our lives without losing our house or the basic foundations of our day-to-day well-being," and "This budget represents a commitment to acknowledging our past, planning for our future, and living life fully in the present." Finally, when they did approach their regular monthly budgeting, they planned it for a time when they were both rested and ready, adding to the task a bit of ritual. They lit a candle, held hands for a moment, and reminded each other that they were in this process together—not as opposing forces. What had once been a dreaded task to push through became a more integral part of their spiritual journey.

If you feel the need to revise your own engagement with the four key money activities, be creative and willing to think outside the box. And don't be opposed to asking for help when you need it! Often, there are many more options than we initially realize—a list of ideas could be as long and as varied as there are people in the world, but here are just a few:

- Change the way you approach your budgeting, as the couple mentioned above did.
- Think before spending money on something an ad says you "need." (Remember the story I mentioned in chapter 1 of me buying the phones!) Try to recognize what you're truly attempting to purchase: happiness, peace of mind, alleviation of fear? Are these things really purchasable? Instead, turn your thoughts toward all the things you already have and are grateful for.
- Consider a job change even though it might take tremendous energy and courage, but don't do it rashly—envision it, work toward it, embrace it when the timing is right. If you are suddenly forced into a job change, look at it as possible blessing in disguise. Think about your courageous vision as you think about next steps.
- Look at your job from a different angle. Maybe there's a different way to approach it: job sharing, asking for less pay and more flexibility, and so on.
- Start giving money to causes that make you feel excited rather than those that make you feel guilty—or volunteer your time instead of your money.

- Think about how and why you tip at a restaurant and how you connect to the person who is serving you. Do you look him or her in the eye?

- Look at your purchasing habits. Do you tend to shop when you're tired, depressed, hungry? Do you go into the store for one thing and end up with twenty? Examine these habits and think how you might change them, not in terms of denying yourself, but by replacing them with habits that support your courageous vision.

- Consider having an honest, two-sided conversation with someone about money. Most people have a subject they know needs to be addressed, but they avoid it or put it off for the opportune moment. Consider the fact that there may never be an opportune time and have the conversation anyway. Maybe it's with your parents about the cost of their elder care or your inheritance. Maybe it's your children about money expectations. Maybe it's a sibling or friend you're having issues with around money. I do recommend—if you are planning to have a conversation—that you run your ideas first by a trusted friend or confidant. Such conversations can be loaded, so it's important to enter them thoughtfully and not reactively. The fact that they are loaded is why they are difficult and, therefore, why it's so important to have them. And of course, be prepared to listen, not just talk.

- Downsize your house and therefore your household expenses. Have you thought about cohousing or other shared living experiences?

- If you have money in investments, talk to a professional about social screenings for those investments. Or find out more about shareholder proxy voting as a way of influencing the companies where your money is invested.
- Keep an eye open for information about financial institutions that support your vision. They do exist!
- Decide you will only shop at certain stores or purchase certain items.
- Devote yourself to reducing, reusing, and recycling.
- Incorporate rituals into your personal financial tasks and include your family members in those rituals.
- Make a commitment to take a five-minute walk instead of buying that extra-large salted-caramel mocha chip whipped-cream-topped latte. Or just make a commitment to buy a small one instead.

The basis of any spiritual practice is just that—practice. It means making changes, maybe tiny, maybe grand, but making them and practicing them, perhaps poorly at first (this is why it's practice) but with devotion. Here is where we want to use courage to change the negative habits we currently have on autopilot. Practicing new habits is hard—we all know that, but if the new practices align with your courageous vision, positive habituation should follow.

CHAPTER 4

Looking Out

Life engenders life. Energy creates energy. It
is by spending oneself that we become rich.

—SARAH BERNHARDT

M y first spiritual practice was Catholicism. My brother Mark and I were born into it and raised by it, and this practice always fed Mark. He went to a Catholic college and attended mass several times a week as an adult. Not me. For many reasons—some of which I've already touched upon in this book—I felt disconnected from the institutional church and couldn't continue down that road.

I had another spiritual practice as a child, though I didn't recognize it as such until I was an adult. When I was young, I loved sitting alone in a willow tree in our front yard. The yard was big, and the tree sat back toward the east side of the house by itself. When I sat in its branches, I could see out, but it seemed (at least to me) that others couldn't see in. I was very lonely as a child, and the tree was a comfort to me. It held me in its arms. It was easy to climb into, and I could sit for hours in the cradle of its branches. It was a quiet, alone time, and as I remember it now, I felt there was a kind of magic in that tree. That was spiritual practice.

For many people, like my brother Mark, spiritual practice can be found in organized religion. For me, I have found it in meditation, spending time in nature, solitude, and connection with other people. (Some days I add beer and football to the mix.) I have tried to incorporate these practices into my adult life, but there is, of course, my profession in the financial industry. Like many people, I was taught growing up that religion went in one pigeonhole and everything else (money for instance) had its own separate space. I no longer believe in those lines. When I started my financial profession, I spent my days talking to people about dollar figures and future plans for those dollars. That was the extent of the conversation by industry standards, but from the beginning, I saw that those figures and plans were woven into something much bigger and much deeper. The conversations around money I was having with people every day intertwined with the larger tapestry of each person's life, including their spiritual lives, yet there was no opportunity to address this. There was not even a framework on which to envision the connection.

Developing this framework has been a focus of my work and life ever since. Many elements have contributed to that development. In chapter 2 I mentioned my fascination with Bill Plotkin's books and his nature-rooted psychology. I have participated in several of Plotkin's Animus Valley Institute programs and found them incredibly valuable. I consider them an element of my own spiritual practice. They have also influenced my thoughts about how people relate to money and the entire economic system. They have helped me see how much our financial system excludes and denies the natural world, and how detrimental that denial is to us as individuals and as a society.

I also mentioned earlier that I became a Certified Money Coach (CMC)® through the Money Coaching Institute with Deborah Price. Today I continue to guide clients as a financial planner through my business, Chicory Wealth, coach individuals through their emotional issues around money, speak to churches and other groups on these issues, lead and participate in spiritual retreats with money and nature as elements, and try to untangle the knots that money creates in my own life, as well as the lives of others.

Not long ago, I had a dream in which I was in the foyer of a large conference room looking through the doors into a banquet hall. I knew there were a lot of people in there, and I would soon be walking in and communicating with them in some way—perhaps I was the speaker. Then I looked down and saw that I was covered in beautiful, shiny gold from head to foot. In the next panel of the dream, I was walking down a street and saw an alley. At the end of the alley was a vault. The door was swung wide open, and I saw it was full of gold. I heard a voice say, "All is hidden in plain sight." For me this dream spoke to my belief that our financial realities should not be hidden or denied, but revealed and tied to our spiritual journey toward wholeness and connection.

Money is, of course, not the only aspect of our lives that has been separated from the spiritual path. In Western culture our standard mode of thinking is dualistic—this or that, yes or no, right or wrong. So our spiritual life is necessarily separate from every other aspect of our life—money, work, sex, and politics, for instance. But the spiritual path teaches us that this segmentation is an illusion. Dissolving that illusion in light of our finances is one step—one that should help us recognize and accept the connection between all aspects of our lives. No part of our lives is devoid of a sacred center, if we can just connect to it.

A particular event in my own life dramatically brought this home to me. I remember vividly the July day in 2015 that I took the call from my nephew, breaking the news that my brother Mark had just been diagnosed with a very aggressive form of brain cancer—a glioblastoma. Mark was fifty-nine years old and had finally retired from the family business just a year or so earlier. For the first time in his life, he was free to enjoy time with his wife and sons, and two young grandchildren. He was volunteering for charities, attending Notre Dame football games, and going to mass several times a week. He also worked out at the gym three times a week and appeared to be in perfect health. The day before my nephew called me, Mark had been driving home from an early morning workout when something happened and he blacked out. He didn't remember how, but miraculously, he pulled his car over to the side of the road where a police officer found him and tapped on the window. Mark was confused, so he was taken to the hospital where he was told he'd suffered a grand mal seizure. It didn't take long to locate the brain tumor. On that gorgeous July day, a quick Google search told me the median survival rate for this type of cancer was fourteen months.

The minute I heard the news, a wave of grief crash over me. He was my closest sibling; I couldn't wrap my head around the news. We were all devastated, asking ourselves the question everyone can't help but ask at times like this: *Why is this happening? It's so unfair.* But there is never an answer to that question. There is no "fair." We all suffer intense sorrows and tragedies throughout our lives and the only "answer" is how we navigate those waters.

Mark's navigation through those waters during the next months was his own, filled with traditional and experimental treatments, all extreme. His devout faith carried him through, and he never lost his sense of humor or compassion for others or himself. Money played a role in his experience, too, of course. He had saved money and had good health insurance, so he was able to have the best treatment possible. He also told me he was glad he had bitten the bullet a few years earlier and purchased long-term care insurance, which allowed him to have in-home care during his illness. Monetarily, his wife and family would be well cared for when he was gone. Would he have traded some of that financial cushion for a few more years of freedom from a job that often frustrated and disheartened him? I don't know, and it's not really a helpful question. All I can speak to is my own experience during that time. I was heartsick with grief, and it forced me to think long and hard about my own work and money-making life. I love my work, but at the time I was putting in grueling hours, some of those hours on tasks I did not much enjoy. Was it worth it? Was it "necessary"? Did the elements of my work align with my courageous vision? I took the opportunity to look deeply at these questions and make some changes.

Always an overachiever, Mark lived seventeen months from the date of his diagnosis. I was crushed by the loss, and the hole he left behind will never completely close. But that deep grief is also part of my own spiritual path, which has grown deeper and more meaningful since his illness and death. I lean into the sorrow I feel and accept it, but try not to drown underneath it. I listen to the lessons his life and death are teaching me—about family, about love, about illness, about humor, about making and saving money, about Notre Dame football—all of it. And I try to discern its connection to the bigger tapestry. It's what we all must do.

Life as Spiritual Practice

My story is unique, as is each person's, but all our stories are similar in that they are filled with pain, mess, joy, laughter, sorrow, peace. Ultimately, we are all part of one story. It's the same with spiritual practice, which is deeply personal and grounded in each person's unique and circuitous journey. But there's a beautiful irony to this individual journey: The goal is to dissolve the illusion that we are separate from each other, from the "outer" world, from the divine. Spiritual practice helps us experience beautiful moments of connection and thus enhance our experiences of compassion, love, empathy, beauty, and a feeling of being "in flow," "in tune," or "at home" with our heart centers and all of reality. This is what we all yearn for.

No one can tell someone else how to enhance these moments of connection, but there are practices that help. This book has been an attempt to bring finances out of its pigeonhole and into the practices that enhance that spiritual connection. The practices I've presented necessarily relate to money—our wounds and joys around money, tendencies and patterns in money activities, talents and desires for the future, the discernment of a courageous vision and its connection to money—and are meant to help you align these aspects of your life with the inner spiritual life. But all of life's "segments" should ultimately dovetail with each other and the spiritual life, not just one or a few. In all aspects of our lives, we need to listen to our inner heart. We must pay attention to our choices and be honest in our responses to what life hands us. We must draw from our experiences and knowledge, experiment with new avenues and ways of thinking, and connect in a real way with each other and the planet. Though there are many ways to reach for this connection, I've included below a partial list of practices that may help you weave together the elements of your life into spiritual alignment, money included.

PRACTICES:

Education

Expand your horizons by reading about or taking workshops on subjects that are nudging you for more attention: Maybe it's a type of artwork or a social subject like racism or sexism. Maybe it's our economy and how it might be transformed, health care in our country, or how climate change is affecting our planet. Perhaps this book has ignited a spark of interest in finance and investing, or you find yourself drawn to spiritual texts new to you. Dive in and learn about what's calling to you. Several resources that might be of interest are in the footnotes section of this book.

Groups

Join discussion groups on a particular subject or focus—a book club, a political group, a spiritual group, and so on. Look for groups that allow you to be yourself and that you can trust. This is not just about intellectual stimulation, but finding a place where you can begin to open up with people about your story and listen to theirs. Establishing this type of group does take time to evolve. When you're sharing in this type of gathering, practice nonjudgmental compassion with yourself and with others.

Symbols

Pay attention to your dreams, symbols you run across in your daily life, and coincidental and uncanny events. I mentioned one of my dreams. I've had many that have guided me along the way. Here's an example from a friend who had a dream a few months after her father died (her mother had died a few years earlier) and she inherited a small amount of money. In the dream, she was in a store purchasing gifts for people and something for herself. At first, this was enjoyable, and she felt happy about it, but soon she began to worry that it was all going to be too expensive and she wouldn't be able to pay for it. As the dream progressed, she began to realize that it wasn't her money after all, but her parents', and this made her feel bad. She worried about what she would tell them and how they would react. The dream switched at this point to a different scene where her father was leading her through a dark and foggy place. They were high up on a wall, and she was afraid of falling. However, her father seemed confident and bold. She found comfort in following him and wished she had his confidence. They came to a massive door that was difficult to open, but somehow her father was able to push the door open, and they walked through. For my friend, this dream was a message that her parents were okay with her enjoying and sharing the money that she had received from them through their deaths.

Uncanny events can also help guide you. I know someone who was struggling with something he had done as a youth that harmed someone else. He had felt guilty about this act for years and finally admitted out loud to someone else that he wished he could somehow make amends to that person. But that was impossible since he hadn't seen the person in more than thirty years and had no idea where he lived. Within two weeks of speaking his desire out loud, the person he had harmed miraculously appeared in his life again, and he was able to make amends. I'm sure you've heard similar stories as well. Pay attention to these symbols in your life. What are they saying to you? What gifts are they offering?

Mindfulness

Mindfulness is perhaps an overused word today, but I believe that's because it is a powerful practice. Mindfulness means being aware of your mind and your body in the here and now. It is the energy of being fully present to the moment. This might take the form of meditating on your breath, taking a slow walk where each step corresponds with a breath, listening to a piece of music without doing something else at the same time, or trying to keep your mind on your daily tasks while you do them. "I am washing the dishes. I am taking a shower. I am walking the dog." Mindfulness is not rocket science, but it's not easy either. It takes practice, so keep practicing it.

Meditation and Centering Prayer

Meditation is a type of mindfulness, and there are many types of meditation. As mentioned above, this may involve focusing on the breath: "I breathe in. I breathe out." When thoughts enter into your mind while meditating, as they surely will, recognize them without judgment and return to the breath. Some also find it helpful to visualize a particular image in their mind's eye and focus on that—perhaps a light or a flower or anything that symbolizes divine love. Meditation can also be in the form of prayer, for example, centering prayer, which is practiced by contemplative Christians. There are different types of centering prayer, but one example is silently focusing the mind on certain words in conjunction with the breath: "Inhale—Beloved. Exhale—Jesus" or "Inhale— God who created the sun. Exhale—You are the sun of my soul. Inhale—And you make me glad. Exhale— Light of the sun be with us today." Use your own words that speak to your heart.

Gifting

Compassion and care for others is a central component of the spiritual path. Spending money for the good of others can help the recipient, but it also helps the person who gives. And it doesn't have to be money, of course. Giving of your time and energy is just as important, if not more so. This will be difficult for some people—either because they are worried about giving too much away or the opposite—they're not giving enough. This is why it's important to go through the practices I laid out in chapter 2 first. It's critically important to give for the right reasons (in other words, as part of your spiritual practice)—not out of guilt or control or denial. I have a friend who says this about giving away her time and energy: "I try to give from my interest, not my principal. If I give away the principal of myself, they'll soon be nothing left."

Positive Habits

We all know that if we want to change a negative habit, the best way is to replace it with a positive habit. The two people I mentioned earlier, who were in the habit of fighting whenever they went over the budget, replaced that negative habit with a positive one of starting each session with a loving ritual. It's also possible to create a positive habit even when you're not replacing something negative. Creating positive habits may be joyful, but getting them to stick certainly takes a commitment. Again, that's why we call it practice.

Here's one example of a person I know who replaced a negative money habit with a positive one: She was in the habit of purchasing books online—especially late at night when she couldn't sleep. She loved books, but realized she was spending way more than she wanted to and didn't even have time to read all the books she purchased. She looked closely at this habit and decided spending money on things she didn't always use did not align with her courageous vision. But she hated giving up the idea of perusing books, which gave her pleasure. A friend suggested she replace online book stores with online libraries. She decided to try it for a couple of months. When she found a book she wanted to read, she could borrow it from the library rather than purchasing it. Not only that but also whenever she borrowed a book rather than purchasing it, she added the cost of the book to a tally to see how much she was saving. She told me that making this switch wasn't necessarily easy and didn't happen overnight. She enjoyed the online library, but at first she was often tempted to go back to shopping. But she reminded herself of the reasons why she was trying out this new habit—and the growing tally of money she was saving gave her more and more motivation. By the time two months came and went, she was truly enjoying her new habit. At the end of a year, she decided to use half of the money she had saved on something for herself, and half went to the Friends of the Library. She said this made her truly happy.

Creating positive habits—whether it's committing to twenty-five or even five minutes of meditation every day, replacing negative and worried voices speaking in your head with positive ones, or pushing yourself to engage in conversations you feel are important, but find difficult—doesn't happen overnight. Many people are tempted to give up because they are not "good enough" at the outset. Dismiss these messages; remember—it's "practice." Challenge yourself in a gentle way and keep going, so you can create habits that feed your connection to spirit and your courageous vision.

Nature

For me, taking ample time in the natural world is a key part of my spiritual practice. I have a regular walking practice, but another good idea is to create an outside "sit spot" you can visit regularly. In your own special spot, you can sit in nature and be quiet, thoughtful, and open to the natural world. Spending time in such places can be incredibly healing. For those who don't have easy access to recreational areas or parks, anything that gets you out of the "indoor bubble" will help. It might be a walk around the block at lunchtime or staring at the stars from your rooftop at night. And when you do get an opportunity to get out in nature—take it. Leave the electronic distractions behind.

Body Practices

All religions have some type of body movement associated with their rituals, although some have more than others. The mind is part of the physical body, so it's important to bring both along on the spiritual path. Don't leave the body behind. Some suggestions include yoga, dancing, walking, martial arts, swimming, or chanting.

Journaling

Journaling on a regular basis is an excellent spiritual practice and might have a particular focus. Gratitude journaling was described in chapter 3. Journals might take the form of letters to God, insights on the spiritual journey (including money), dream tracking, poetry, or stream of consciousness writing, to name a few. It can also be insightful to look back over your journals from time to time to see where you have been at different points along your path. You may be surprised at how far you've come.

Creativity

Getting lost in some type of artwork can be a kind of mindfulness, as well as opening a door to the psyche. Examples include painting, collage, poetry, music, drawing, coloring, sculpture, weaving, woodwork, even doodling. This may not initially appeal to those who were told when they were young that they weren't creative or had no natural "talent," but I suggest saying to those voices, "Thanks for sharing, but you can move along now." The goal of creativity in spiritual practice is not a beautiful byproduct by someone else's standards, but the creation process itself. Artwork may also be a message from yourself. When you are finished, step back and look. What are your creations saying to you?

Food

The preparation, consumption, and clean-up of our food can be a mundane task. But it is a task we do every single day and, therefore, a wonderful opportunity for practice. Think about all these aspects of your food life and whether they are aligned with your courageous vision. If not, what could be changed? What positive habits could you create to help these tasks feed not only your body, but your spirit, and the spirit of the wider world?

Solitude and Community

People need both solitude and community—the amounts of each vary by person, but both are needed. Figure out how you can have both in your life. If you find yourself craving solitude in a life busy with people and tasks, listen to that call and try to create even small moments of solitude for yourself. But community is important too. By this, I don't mean just being around people. Some people (many people at times) actually drain us, rather than feed us. It's important to connect with a community of others that gives you strength, wisdom, and accountability. These communities will be different for different people—maybe it's a religious group, a meditation group, an intentional community, a twelve-step program, or a civic or volunteer organization. The important ingredient for walking the spiritual path is finding a group that supports your values in a healthy way—where you feel at home and fed, rather than depleted.

The Heart

Faith is taking the first step even when
you don't see the whole staircase.
—MARTIN LUTHER KING JR.

B ut what about the whale?
Integrating money into our spiritual practice will
necessarily change our connection to and experiences
within our whale of a monetary system, but will it change the
whale? I don't know the answer to that question, but I have a
strong sense that it will, or at least that it can.

For one thing, the growing movement toward alternative
economies gives me hope. I'm encouraged by the interest in
relationship- and people-centered economies that is growing
in the United States and around the world. There is a new focus
on reduced consumerism and requiring businesses to pay
for "externalities" (environmental and other costs associates
with a business but aren't paid by that business). I see a rise
in socially responsible investing, financial literacy in public
education, shared consumption businesses, and ecological and

green industries. This movement is made up of people like E.F. Schumacher, who wrote the 1973 book *Small Is Beautiful: A Study of Economics as if People Mattered*; Herman Daly and the Center for the Advancement of the Steady State Economy; environmentalist, entrepreneur, and author of numerous books Paul Hawken; Van Jones, who wrote *The Green Collar Economy*; David C. Korten, author of several books, including *When Corporations Rule the World* and *Change the Story, Change the Future: A Living Economy for a Living Earth*; and numerous other authors, as well as many organizations and foundations working toward change in this field.[1]

One of the strongest voices in this movement is speaker and author Charles Eisenstein, who has written numerous publications on his courageous vision for a new and more positive money system. In 2008 he wrote this about that vision, which he called "the Age of Reunion":

> Money in the Age of Reunion will be an agent for the development of social, cultural, natural, and spiritual capital, and not their consumption. It will be a mechanism for the sharing of wealth and not its accumulation. It will be a means for the creation of beauty, not its diminishment. It will be a barrier to greed and not an incentive. It will encourage joyful creative work, and not necessitate "jobs." It will reinforce the cyclical processes of nature, and not violate them. And it will accompany a shift in consciousness that we are beginning to experience today, a shift toward a connected self in love with the world. That, after

all, is the true self, and that is what we will return
to as the pretense of everlasting increase collapses.[2]

Eisenstein has continued to refine his theories for a
renewed monetary system over the years and has a substantial following. His 2011 book *Sacred Economics: Money, Gift, and Society in the Age of Transition* describes our culture's modern capitalist system, which is based on competition, a framework of scarcity, and the need for unending growth. This path is clearly not sustainable, as we're all beginning to realize. He offers his ideas for transitioning to a more sustainable "gift" economy, or "a more beautiful world our hearts tell us is possible." If you consider such an idea a utopian fantasy or an idealistic pipedream, you may be limiting the power of your spiritual path. Eisenstein says this in *Sacred Economics*:

> Fantastical? The mind is afraid to hope for anything too good. If this description evokes anger, despair, or grief, then it has touched our common wound, the wound of separation. Yet the knowledge of what is possible lives on inside each of us, inextinguishable. Let us trust this knowing, hold each other in it, and organize our lives around it. Do we really have any choice, as the old world falls apart? Shall we settle for anything less than a sacred world?[3]

In spite of this optimism, many will argue that the whale doesn't show any signs of changing. In fact, it seems to grow more bloated each day. The United States' current political and economic direction is a prime example. The predominant assumption today in the United States is that the country should be run like a for-profit corporation. That's part of the reason a billionaire TV show host is the current president and social programs that don't "make money" are being slashed. We can't pretend that this mind-set isn't running roughshod over all of us here and many other parts of the world. It's easy to believe that there's no way to reverse such an entrenched system—a system seemingly without a heart or any interest in long-term communal health.

But that is the beauty and mystery of spiritual practice. We do not have to see the whole road toward a changed system, and in fact, we never will. Our focus is our own practice. When it comes to money, we can learn to address our history, practices, and dysfunction, and to search for meaning in our money activities and their connection to the broader world. We can educate ourselves about alternative economies and how we might support them. We can learn to be more honest with ourselves about our choices and how they shape others and the planet. We can stop running from fear and address our privilege and the very impulses in ourselves that we may be critiquing in the wider culture. Through spiritual practice our posture will begin to take on the shape of empathy, compassion, and a sense of interconnectedness. Our choices and relationships will necessarily take on this shape as well.

Most of us by now have heard the old story the grandmother tells her grandchild. She describes for the child the two wolves fighting inside the young girl. One wolf is filled with fear, anger, resentment, pride, envy, and greed. The other is filled with serenity, harmony, joy, kindness, and generosity.

When the child asks which will win, the grandmother says, "The one you feed."

Spiritual practice is feeding that part of ourselves that is oriented toward serenity, harmony, truth, compassion, gratitude, love, and joy. It's a letting go of our dual presumptions of black and white, yes and no, right and wrong, have and have not, and a falling into a third place we might call "divine flow," or "heart center," or "home." It's the place the desert mothers and fathers of the third century yearned for and the reason they lived in solitude praying, fasting, laboring, and denouncing material goods. It's the same for the monastics who have followed them and for anyone who longs for unity with the divine—whether they sense that divine within themselves, somewhere above, or connected in all things and everywhere—and begins to take the steps to get there, however small those steps may be.

Will our personal spiritual practice make any difference to the wider money system? I don't know. But I do know the "system" does not come from nowhere. It comes from a collective consciousness, which our individual consciousness feeds. We and the system we inhabit are connected to and influenced by each other. Our own practice necessarily affects the people and institutions around us. This is the premise of many religious traditions, and has recently been studied by the scientific community. As just one example, this is the subject of *The Book of Joy*, a discussion between His Holiness the Dalai Lama and Archbishop Desmond Tutu on cultivating joy and happiness. Joy is contagious, they say. When we feel joy, others do too; in fact, joy in its purest form emerges by turning not toward yourself, but toward others and recognizing their joy. The narrator of the discussion, Douglas Abrams, describes it this way:

> The goal is not just to create joy for ourselves, but as the Archbishop poetically phrased it, "To be a reservoir of joy, an oasis of peace, a pool of serenity that can ripple out to all those around you."⁴

What these spiritual leaders are describing is a spiritual practice focused on joy. And it is a holistic practice; nothing can be segmented or left behind. Not even money. Adding money to our spiritual path will help us more easily inhabit the money system skillfully, even sacredly, without being undone by it. We will start to live with less need to protect our power or live in the house of scarcity and fear. Beyond that—we'll see. I'm paraphrasing here, but the Gnostic gospels proclaim, "As the inner, so the outer." Our own hearts are the heart of the whale. Our path is the journey to that heart—a place of joy, meaning, and true wealth.

Footnotes and Resources

Chapter 1

1. Charles Eisenstein, *Sacred Economics: Money, Gift, and Society in the Age of Transition*, Transcribed talk from 1/13/12 at "The Hive" in Vancouver, BC, http://charleseisenstein.net/sacred-economics-money-the-gift-and-society-in-the-age-of-transition/.
2. Vicki Robin and Joe Dominguez, *Your Money or Your Life: 9 Steps to Transforming Your Relationship with Money and Achieving Financial Independence* (New York, Penguin Books, 1992).
3. Mark Fahey, "Money Can Buy Happiness But Only Up To A Point," CNBC, 12/14/15, http://www.cnbc.com/2015/12/14/money-can-buy-happiness-but-only-to-a-point.html.
4. Paul Piff, "Does Money Make You Mean?" TED TALK, October 2013, https://www.ted.com/talks/paul_piff_does_money_make_you_mean; and Drake Baer, "Rich People Literally See the World Differently," New York Magazine, 2/14/17, http://nymag.com/scienceofus/2017/02/how-rich-people-see-the-world-differently.html.

5. St. Augustine of Hippo, *Confessions,* 400.

6. Blaise Pascal, *Pensées,* 1662.

7. Elizabeth Chmurak, "Dr. Deepak Chopra on 2016 Race: Trump Brings Out Our 'Dark Side'," Fox Business, 3/24/16, http://www.foxbusiness.com/politics/2016/03/24/dr-deepak-chopra-on-2016-race-trump-brings-out-our-dark-side.html .

8. Tim Wise, *Under the Affluence: Shaming the Poor, Praising the Rich and Sacrificing the Future of America* (City Lights Publishers, 2015).

9. Here are some resources on income inequality in our society:

   • Dennis Kucinich, "Our Political Economy Is Designed to Create Poverty and Inequality," The Nation 3/6/17, www.thenation.com/article/our-political-economy-is-designed-to-create-poverty-and-inequality/.

   • David Roberts, "None of the World's Top Industries Would Be Profitable If They Paid for the Natural Capital They Use," Grist, 4/17/13, http://grist.org/business-technology/none-of-the-worlds-top-industries-would-be-profitable-if-they-paid-for-the-natural-capital-they-use/.

   • "State of Working America Key Numbers: Inequality," Economic Policy Institute, http://www.stateofworkingamerica.org/fact-sheets/inequality-facts/.

   • David C. Korten, *Change the Story, Change the Future: A Living Economy for a Living Earth* (Berrett-Korhler Publishers, Inc., 2015 by the Living Economies Forum).

10. Suzanne Woolley, "Are Young Americans Ashamed of Their Debt?" Bloomberg, 2/7/17, https://www.bloomberg.com/news/articles/2017-02-07/40-of-millennials-prefer-to-tell-a-date-about-an-std-than-debt.

Chapter 2

1. Deborah L. Price, Money Coaching Institute, http://moneycoachinginstitute.com/understanding-money-types/.
2. Deborah L. Price, *Money Magic: Unleashing Your True Potential for Prosperity and Fulfillment* (New World Library, 2003).
3. Sandra E. Black, Paul J. Devereux, Petter Lundborg, Kaveh Majlesi, "Poor Little Rich Kids? The Determinants of the Intergenerational Transmission of Wealth" (National Bureau of Economic Research: Working Paper No. 21409, Issued in July 2015), www.nber.org/papers/w21409 .
4. Dan Hurley, "Grandma's Experiences Leave a Mark on Your Genes," Discover Magazine, May 2013, http://discovermagazine.com/2013/may/13-grandmas-experiences-leave-epigenetic-mark-on-your-genes.
5. Bill Plotkin, *Nature and the Human Soul: Cultivating Wholeness and Community in a Fragmented World* (New World Library, 2007).
6. Bill Plotkin, *Wild Mind: A Field Guide to the Human Psyche* (New World Library, 2013).

Chapter 3

1. George Kinder, *The Seven Stages of Money Maturity* (Dell Publishers, 2000).
2. Quoted by David C. Korten in his book *Change the Story, Change the Future: A Living Economy for a Living Earth* (Berrett-Korhler Publishers, Inc., 2015 by the Living Economies Forum), page 16.
3. Martin Luther King Jr., as quoted by the King Center, http://the kingcenter.org/blog/mlk-quote-week-faith-taking-first-step.
4. Eckhart Tolle, *A New Earth: Awakening to Your Life's Purpose* (Penguin Books, 2005), page 58.
5. Christina Prignano, "Jason Chaffetz says people should invest in health care instead of buying iPhones," Boston Globe, 3/7/17, www.bostonglobe.com/news/politics/2017/03/07/jason-chaffetz-says-people-should-invest-health-care-instead-buying-iphones/AMInYg6r SoZzVu8Q0uhrxK/story.html.
6. Positive Psychology Program, April 5, 2014, quoting Elizabeth W. Dunn, Lara B. Aknin, Michael I. Norton's report, "How Spending Money on Others Promotes Happiness," University of British Columbia, Harvard Business School 2008, https://positivepsychologyprogram.com/spending-money-promotes-happiness/ .

Chapter 5

1. Here is a small list of some of the publications and organizations involved in the alternative economies movement:

- E. F. Schumacher, *Small Is Beautiful: A Study of Economics as if People Mattered* (Harper Perennial; Reprint edition, 2010; original publication 1973)
- Paul Hawken, *Natural Capitalism: Creating the Next Industrial Revolution* (US Green Building Council, 2000), and *The Ecology of Commerce, A Declaration of Sustainability* (HarperBusiness, Revised edition 2010; original publication 1993)
- Van Jones, *The Green Collar Economy: How One Solution Can Fix Our Two Biggest Problems* (HarperOne, 2008)
- David C. Korten, *When Corporations Rule the World* (Berrett-Koehler Publishers, Inc.; 3rd edition 2015; original publication 1995) and *Change the Story, Change the Future: A Living Economy for a Living Earth* (Berrett-Korhler Publishers, Inc., 2015 by the Living Economies Forum)
- Charles Eisenstein, "Money: A New Beginning (Part 2)" 4/18/08 http://realitysandwich.com/1369/money_a_new_beginning_part_2/
- Center for a New Economics, www.centerfor neweconomics.org
- Center for the Advancement of the Steady State Economy, www.steadystate.org
- New Dream (formerly Center for a New American Dream), www.newdream.org
- Partners for a New Economy, www.p4ne.org

2. Charles Eisenstein, "Money: A New Beginning (Part 2)" 4/18/08 http://realitysandwich.com/1369/money_a_new_beginning_part_2/.

3. Charles Eisenstein, 2011 *Sacred Economics: Money, Gift, and Society in the Age of Transition* (North Atlantic Books, 2011) Chapter 24, http://sacred-economics.com/sacred-economics-chapter-24-conclusion-the-more-beautiful-world-our-hearts-tell-us-is-possible/.
4. His Holiness the Dalai Lama and Archbishop Desmond Tutu, with Douglas Abrams, *The Book of Joy: Lasting Happiness in a Changing World,* audiobook (Penguin Audio, 2016 The Dalai Lama Trust), Disc 2, Track 5.

Made in the USA
Columbia, SC
16 March 2019